Beyond Abuse

Achieve Healing Through Spiritual Practices

Author's Disclaimer
This book depicts actual events in my life as truthfully as recollection permits. I changed individuals' names and some geographic locations to respect their privacy. The events are meant to provide context for the spiritual treatments I describe. I, Christopher Paul Russell, am not a medical doctor, nor do I practice medicine. I do not diagnose, cure, heal, or treat disease. The spiritual treatments described in this book reflect my own experiences, and individual results based on these treatments may vary. These treatments are not a substitute for conventional medical or psychological diagnoses or treatments.

Publisher's Disclaimer
This book is a memoir. It reflects the author's present recollections of experiences over time. Although the author, editor, and publisher have made every effort to ensure accuracy, we do not assume and hereby disclaim any liability to any party for any loss, damage, or disruption caused by errors or omissions, whether such errors or omissions result from negligence, accident, or any other cause. This book is not intended as a substitute for the professional advice of physicians and therapists.

Beyond Abuse: Achieve Healing Through Spiritual Practices
Copyright © 2023, Christopher Paul Russell

All rights reserved.
No part of this book may be reproduced in any form without permission in writing from the publisher, except for brief quotations embodied in critical articles or reviews.

Park Point Press
573 Park Point Drive
Golden, CO 80401-7402
720-496-1370

www.csl.org/publications/books
www.scienceofmind.com/publish-your-book

Printed in the United States of America
Published April 2023

Cover Illustration: Bobbye Overman
Editor: Julie Mierau, JM Wordsmith
Design/Layout: Maria Robinson, Designs On You, LLC

ISBN paperback: 978-1-956198-25-6
ISBN ebook: 978-1-956198-26-3

Christopher writes a sincere, sensitive, and spiritually grounding work in his debut book, Beyond Abuse. His readers will be touched by his honesty as well as his transformational journey. I am confident this wonderful book will bless many thousands of people who are searching to heal from their own painful pasts. He ushers them in to a future of grace, freedom, and possibility by shining his light through this wonderful book.
— *Dr. Roger Teel*
Senior Minister Emeritus, Mile Hi Church, Lakewood, Colorado

As someone who has experienced his own childhood trauma and who has spent much of his professional career providing treatment for those who have suffered from trauma, I highly recommend the book Beyond Abuse by Christopher Russell. In this book, Christopher poignantly and powerfully describes the physical and psychological abuses of his childhood. As an adult, he had the courage to face the pain of those abuses and then put them in perspective. The title of his book, Beyond Abuse, is appropriate because he has not only been able to write about the abuse but also has used those experiences to grow, both psychologically and spiritually, and to describe practices that helped him and are likely to help others. Now that he has become a Religious Science practitioner, his personal growth will allow him to benefit the colleagues and clients who have the good fortune to work with him. His sons are fortunate to have such a loving and courageous father.
— *Richard Koken, M.D.*
Diplomate of the American Board of Psychiatry and Neurology in Adult and Child Psychiatry

In Beyond Abuse, Christopher Russell shares his journey and the great awakening that emerged within him with clarity, compassion, and a deep conviction that healing is available to everyone who awakens to the higher reality they espouse. Follow his road map and you'll feel the weight of shame and regret fall away and a new gloriously bright life emerge within you.
— *Rev. Dr. John B. Waterhouse*
Co-founding Minister, Center for Spiritual Living, Asheville, North Carolina

Christopher Russell's book provides powerful real world experience of the challenges faced from experiencing an abusive childhood met with healing ideas and techniques to thrive beyond abuse. That perfect recipe calls forth great hope and healing. What a joy.
— *Rev. Dr. Michelle Medrano*
Senior Minister, Mile Hi Church, Lakewood, Colorado

Because I know the author, I have seen these principles at work in his life through his focused attention and awareness. I am grateful he has summarized and condensed the practices that helped him overcome the traumatic impacts of abuse into a guide for the rest of us. Christopher's story is a dramatic example of how hurt people hurt people, and he does an incredible job of demonstrating and explaining how any of us — no matter the scope or extent of our own trauma — can heal ourselves through changing our own perceptions and limiting beliefs.

— **Tracy Maxwell**
Book Coach and Author of Being Single, With Cancer: A Solo Survivor's Guide to Life, Love, Health & Happiness

"Developing self-awareness requires us to go within, and going within is both one of the most challenging and one of the most rewarding tasks we can undertake." Christopher Russell shares this not just as sage advice in Beyond Abuse, *but by example over and over through incredibly honest sharing, self-reflection, and clearly tested spiritual practices that helped him heal and grow beyond abuse. Truly, his example will be a healing inspiration for others to follow.*

— **Rev. Josh Reeves**
Senior Minister, Mile Hi Church, Lakewood, Colorado

In Beyond Abuse, *Christopher Russell tells a frank and personally revealing story of the challenges of his life, ultimately leading us to the spiritual practices that assisted in his personal growth. At the heart of his healing was the life-changing New Thought philosophy of Science of Mind. At the heart of his book is the message that when we let go of being a victim to our story, we are all empowered to create the lives we truly want.*

— **Rev. Mark Gilbert**
Author of Be Yourself: Evolving the World Through Personal Empowerment

Beyond Abuse

Achieve Healing Through Spiritual Practices

CHRISTOPHER PAUL RUSSELL,
RSCP

Park Point
PRESS

Park Point Press is an imprint of Centers for Spiritual Living
573 Park Point Drive | Golden CO 80401

DEDICATION

This book is dedicated to all those who are on the path of using the traumatic and challenging experiences in their lives to discover the gifts found in the healing journey, and who generously share their stories of personal growth and healing with the world to uplift the lives of others. It is also dedicated to all those who are just beginning to consciously engage in their own journeys of healing from past traumas, as they seek to uplift their lives and the lives of those around them.

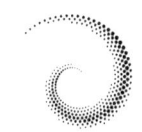

TABLE OF CONTENTS

Dedication vii
Acknowledgments xiii
Foreword xv
Introduction xvii
An Introduction to Science of Mind xxiii

PART ONE
MY LIFE AND MY STORY 1

Chapter 1 — HONORING THE ABUSE 7
   Abuse Disguised as Games 9
   Abuse Disguised as Discipline 12
   Verbal and Emotional Abuse 16
   Abuse from My Mother 17
   Violence Between My Parents 20
   Insufficient Closure 22

Chapter 2 — THE NEED TO FEEL OUR EMOTIONS 25

Chapter 3 — RELEASE THE RESENTMENT
             AND FORGIVE 33
   Forgiveness Is Not Forgetting 36
   Forgiveness Is Not Condoning 43
   Forgiveness Is Not Getting on a High Horse 56

Chapter 4 — SETTING AND MAINTAINING
             HEALTHY BOUNDARIES 61

A New Relationship 64
How I Attracted this Relationship 66
The Relationship Dynamics 67
My Wake-up Call for the Need to Set Healthy Boundaries ... 71
My Forgiveness Process with Anna 73
The Need for Boundaries in All Our Relationships 75

Chapter 5 — HEAL THE PAIN AND SHED
                THE ADDICTIONS 83

My Struggles with Addiction 89
Addiction's Influence in My Romantic Relationships 93
Uprooting My Pain 99
The Effects of My Healing 103
Author's Note for Treating Addiction 105

Chapter 6 — DEVELOP SELF-AWARENESS 107

Identifying and Becoming Aware of Our Ego 110
My Journey of Self-Awareness 112
The Benefits of Going Within 119

PART TWO

THE SPIRITUAL PRACTICES 123

Chapter 7 — MEDITATION 127

My Experience with Meditation 129
Induction Techniques 131
Recognizing the Induction State 139
How to Use Meditation for Healing 143

Chapter 8 — CONSCIOUS PRAYER 155
    Step One: Purpose 162
    Step Two: Recognition 163
    Step Three: Unification............................ 165
    Step Four: Realization............................. 167
    Step Five: Thanksgiving 169
    Step Six: Release 170
    Other Methods of Prayer 174
    Focus Your Prayers on Yourself Only 177

Chapter 9 — CONSCIOUS WRITING 179
    Journaling as a Spiritual Practice 181
    Writing Out Your Limiting Core Beliefs 184
    Dream Journaling as a Spiritual Practice 186
    The Benefits of Writing as a Spiritual Practice 188
    Writing Out New and Beneficial Beliefs 190

Chapter 10 — CONSCIOUS RELATIONSHIPS 193
    My Support Network of Male Mentors 196
    Authenticity in Our Relationships 205
    Non-Conditional Relating 207

Chapter 11 — CONSCIOUS SERVICE.................... 211
    Using Our Gifts for Conscious Service 216
    Expressing Our Gifts through Authentic Sharing 218
    My Discovery and Use of Writing as a Gift 221

Closure: Our Next Generation 225
Bibliography 230
About the Author 233

ACKNOWLEDGMENTS

I thank everyone who provided me with support and encouragement to not only write this book, but to push it forward to completion and to publish it. I am most grateful to my spiritual community, Mile Hi Church in Lakewood, Colorado, its ministers, and the larger global organization of Centers for Spiritual Living. Through using the tools, teachings, and practices embodied by this spiritual community and its teachers, I embarked on my own healing journey and completely changed my life for the better.

I thank the Men's Group at Mile Hi Church, the New Thought Men's Community, and everyone within these groups who supported me in completing this work. A special thanks is necessary for several male mentors in my life who have been with me since the beginning, when I consciously chose to engage in my healing journey: Michael Blevins, Dick Koken, Tom Cowing, Kurt Hopwood, Mark Lewis, and the late Bruce Barton. All of you have been role models, mentors, brothers, and father figures to me, and I am so grateful for your continued presence in my life.

I thank all those who read the initial drafts of this book and provided me with much valuable feedback and encouragement. I offer a special thanks to my first editor, Raven Moore Amerman, who meticulously went through every word of my manuscript and helped me create a much higher quality product while keeping my intentions for the stories and content intact. I greatly appreciate your encouragement to put this out into the world as a published work.

I offer thanks to the countless close friends, prayer partners, and practitioner colleagues who offered their support and encouragement over the years as I completed this. Tracy Maxwell is the first author I met who took the most challenging circumstance in her life and used the good in it to help countless others; you inspired me to do the same. I thank my prayer partner and spiritual brother, Tyler Pollesh, who continued to believe in me, provided prayer support, and encouraged me through this journey. I also thank my prayer partners and spiritual sisters Jackee Leonard and Carrie Sanders, who have done the same. There are many other people who believed in my writing gift and who supported me on this path with encouragement over the years. You all know who you are, and I thank you all for your support and faith in me.

FOREWORD

In this debut book, Christopher Russell openly describes his fear-dominated young life and how he came to recognize his own emotional, mental, and physical expressions and reactions resulting from his experiences of abuse as a child. He narrates how his experiences of severe forms of physical abuse affected his home life, relationships, and marriages as an adult. He openly shares how the damage from his past experiences ultimately brought him to a breaking point, which opened him to consciously choose to heal and break through the patterns of abuse.

Christopher courageously embarked on his journey within using meditation and prayer, and he felt called to express his feelings and engage in his healing process through the gift of writing and journaling. He leads his reader to discover how forgiveness can soften our anxieties, release past resentments, and let go of hurtful judgments. He demonstrates that through changing our perceptions, we can show up with greater authenticity and honesty and engage in healthier relationships, which can be the greatest teachers of all to expand our consciousness.

Christopher shares how the activation of spiritual practices has continued to lead him through impactful and positive changes in his life. No longer is conflict viewed as a reason to turn away from loving someone. He shows us healthy ways to affect change, and he demonstrates how we can consciously work with this great shapeshifter we call change. *Beyond Abuse* is a reflective work that provides an intimate sharing of our relationship with ourselves and our relationships with others. This impactful book is a guide for awakening, with an emphasis on maintaining consistent spiritual practices, to love ourselves through maintaining healthy boundaries, and to live from the awareness of our True Self.

—Dr. Patty Luckenbach
Associate Minister, Mile Hi Church, Lakewood, Colorado

INTRODUCTION

I started journaling in October 2015, shortly after I began attending a church that taught Science of Mind principles. In January 2016, understanding the intricacies of setting conscious intentions and knowing full well what I was doing, I wrote an entry into my journal to the effect that I have long had a desire to help people. I knew my career path as a geotechnical engineer would not give me the opportunities to truly help people in the manner I was feeling called to do. I wanted to help people heal, but I had no idea what that looked like, how it would come about, what I was supposed to do, what path I was supposed to take, or even what exactly I was being called to heal in others.

So I started by writing the intention that I have the desire and I know I also have the ability to help people heal. I wrote a prayer that the details, the resources, the people, and the guidance to make my path clear would show up, and I would allow this process to unfold and would follow it.

I immediately enrolled in classes at my church to pursue practitioner training. I knew this was part of my path the minute I walked through the doors of this church and understood what our prayer practitioners did. I understood they worked with others to provide them with guidance to use spiritual principles more effectively, to help them on their healing journeys, and also to provide them with prayer support during difficult times. I could not deny my calling, and taking that step into the classes was the perfect way to begin.

Over the next year, through the classes and through our Men's Ministry, I started receiving a significant amount of feedback about my writing. I often shared my journal entries with the Men's Ministry, and I also wrote short essays on topics of self-reflection for my classes. I repeatedly heard people tell me that I was a gifted writer, that I needed to continue writing, and that I needed to get my writing out into the world. I then started praying about writing because I had no idea what to write. I had never been a writer, aside from writing my graduate thesis and engineering reports for my profession. What on Earth could I possibly write?

As those of us who have used Science of Mind principles for a significant amount of time can attest, the answers show up on their own once we set the intentions. They often appear in quite unexpected ways when we are open and receptive.

For me, a clear answer showed up in March 2017, as I was driving my children to daycare. My older son, Dillon, seven years old at the time, blurted out to me from the back seat of my truck, completely out of nowhere, "Daddy, you should write a book about the things you put into your journals." My physical and metaphysical ears were wide open, and I heard and felt this pronouncement as if it came directly from God. I now understand fully the absolute truth, which is the pronouncement did come from God, expressing through my son. This was not the first time in my life when I mulled over or prayed about a heavy decision, only to have my son randomly blurt out something directly related to the path I needed to take. He is quite gifted, and I listened to him.

I meditated for a week on what I could write, and then I began writing a bulleted list in my journal. As the topics began downloading into me, I realized I could write a chapter on every bullet point I listed. I also realized other chapters would become apparent once I started the process.

This book is the product of the intention I set years ago to help people in their healing journeys. I maintained this intention as I wrote every word within these pages. I want to share the story of how this path became clear to me, because when my son spoke those words to me, this was one of those inexplicable and special moments when I felt there is a lot more going on around us than meets the eye. I believe I was meant to go through my life experiences, and I was meant to heal from them so I could share my journey. I believe writing is a gift that enables me to share with others, helping as many people on their healing journeys as I can.

I included the words "spiritual practices" in the title so you understand how to use the contents to better your life. Most important to understanding this book is the concept of spiritual practices. I have heard many ministers at my church say, "We call them spiritual *practices* for good reason—we have to practice them regularly for them to be effective." They also refer to them as practices because, quite literally, like any worthwhile skill, we must constantly practice them to improve our abilities and to experience recognizable progress.

Making any profound, lasting changes requires a regular spiritual practice. The changes I made in doing this work have proven to be well worth the effort, and I still need to continue. I came to a point in my life when I realized I needed to make a commitment and carve out time for myself on a daily basis to accomplish the goals I had in mind. I was tired of carrying around all the baggage and garbage associated with being abused as a child. I realized these things I carried with me did not serve me in life; rather, they were a handicap, limitations I imposed on myself and allowed to persist, and I wanted to heal and move on.

It is my hope as you read this book, you also will arrive at a realization that your self-care and healing should be your highest priority in life. I hope you will make a determined decision and a firm commitment to carve out time, ideally on a daily basis, to get the most you can from this material. This is a gift you give to yourself, and you deserve it. This is a means to improve your view and image of yourself, which will improve your life, your health and wellness, your relationships, your enjoyment of hobbies, and your career. And this improvement will be permanent.

This book has two parts. The first part shares much of my life story, beginning with my experiences of childhood abuse and an expression of the painful emotions I suppressed for much of my life related to these experiences. In the next several chapters, I discuss my recognition of how limiting beliefs and suppressed emotions played out in my life and relationships in undesirable ways, recognizing that most victims of abuse likely experience similar challenges. I weave in my personal experiences to share the effects of carrying resentment and then shifting to forgiveness of our abusers, how being a victim of abuse resulted in challenges in learning how to set and maintain healthy boundaries in my relationships, how I used pleasure seeking to cope with the pain and the resulting challenge of working through addiction issues, and finally how I began introspection work to develop self-awareness of all of these dynamics.

The stories I share in my narratives are true, and many of them are intense. I have included them so you can understand that I have been in the same trenches and gone through similar experiences as you. Several therapists over the years told me that I have gone through an intense amount of trauma in my life, particularly in my childhood. Reading my stories may bring up unwanted traumatic memories and painful emotions in you, which may be difficult to deal with. I encourage you to be mindful of this when you are reading through these stories.

If emotions arise within you that begin affecting your day-to-day life or abilities to live as you normally would, or if those emotions cannot be managed effectively, then I recommend you seek out assistance through a licensed therapist, counselor, or mental health specialist. I certainly had to see many of my own through the years, and they provide compassionate listening and effective tools to help us navigate and manage these challenging emotions as we do our healing work.

The second part of the book discusses several spiritual practices I used to accomplish this work. It provides descriptions and instructions to employ practices like meditation, prayer, journaling, maintaining a support network of healthy relationships, and engaging with one's unique gifts in the world —all for the purposes of healing.

The primary goal of this book is to help readers learn how to recognize the limiting core beliefs we have adopted that shape our view or essence of ourselves. Our core beliefs are typically buried deep within our subconscious, and we may not even be aware of them. Whether we are aware of them or not, and whether we want them to or not, our core beliefs influence nearly every aspect of our lives: relationships, spirituality, child rearing, health and wellness, careers, and the level of success or failure we experience in each of these areas.

AN INTRODUCTION TO SCIENCE OF MIND

I attend a church that teaches a spiritual philosophy called Science of Mind. The most fundamental principle in Science of Mind is that we have the power to create our realities and our lives with our thoughts and beliefs. Science of Mind teaches there is a universal Power that interconnects and moves through everything, which responds in a completely unbiased manner to our beliefs, manifesting experiences in our lives directly related to them. We are continually drawing in circumstances that reinforce the beliefs we carry within us.

Science of Mind refers to this universal power as the Law. It is often described using an analogy of soil, and our thoughts and beliefs are compared to seeds. If we plant a specific type of seed, the soil will grow that specific type of plant. The Law responds to our thoughts and beliefs in the same manner. If we continually send out a signal with our beliefs that we are a failure, we will continually have experiences come to us to reinforce and prove that we are a failure, and we will subconsciously seek out situations in which we are likely to experience failure.

The same is true for the opposite. If we continually send out a signal or belief that we are successful in our every endeavor, then success is sure to come to us, and we will seek out situations or draw in experiences in which we experience success.

The truth in this principle requires little stretching of our logic or imagination. I understood this before I ever heard of Science of Mind or started attending this church. I have never heard a story of an Olympic gold medalist, a champion athlete, or a hugely successful business owner who reported achieving their success by holding a negative attitude about themselves or their goals. These individuals share a common trait: They constantly work toward their goals with an unwavering belief they can overcome any obstacle and be successful. There is power in positive thought and beliefs; similarly, there is power in negative thought.

However, thought alone does not have the power to create. Rather, it is thought coupled with emotion, thought coupled with a deeply held conviction, a deep knowing, a *belief*, that has the power to create. We can trick ourselves into thinking positively all day every day, but if the deeply held conviction is not there, if there is no true emotion behind the thoughts, if there is no belief, we will accomplish nothing with our thinking alone.

The particular religion or spirituality you hold has no bearing on this principle. Faith traditions from many cultures recognize this in one form or another. The Bible quotes Jesus Christ as stating, "According to your faith, let it be done for you" (Matthew 9:29, International Standard Version). A similar quote reads, "As you have believed, so let it be done for you" (Matthew 8:13, The New King James Version). There are Buddhist quotes of the same nature: "The mind is the basis for everything. Everything is created by my mind, and is ruled by my mind" (*The Dhammapada*). "With our thoughts we make the world" (*The Dhammapada*). The Bhagavad Gita states, "A man consists of the faith that is in him. Whatever his faith is, he is."

Most major religious traditions also teach the importance of the power of faith—or the power of our beliefs and where we place them. I have personally chosen the principles of Science of Mind because they resonate with me and have worked well in my life. But the practices I put forth in this book have no bearing on any religious or spiritual tradition. Anyone of any religious tradition, or someone with no particular religious tradition, can use these practices to improve their life.

So how does abuse factor into this principle—the idea that we create our reality/lives with our thoughts and beliefs? The fact is, experiences of prolonged, repetitive abuse, particularly as children, shape the core beliefs we adopt and hold onto in our lives. In taking classes at my church and by working with therapists, I learned most humans pick up the majority of our subconscious core beliefs by the time we are age seven. Those of us who have lived through and experienced prolonged abuse as children, or even as adults at the hands of a spouse or partner, likely share an unfortunate commonality: *We have adopted and now live with very limiting core beliefs about ourselves, and these beliefs handicap our experiences and impose limitations on the enjoyment of our lives.*

From my experience, and in talking with others who share a similar history, most of us do not become aware of the effects of these core beliefs until later in life. There is an unfortunate reality that some people never recognize them and instead struggle with them until they pass away. I did not become aware of this fact or recognize its effects in my life until recently, in my early to mid-thirties. If we accept and understand this principle—that we create our lives/realities with our beliefs—then the urgency to identify, recognize, and heal the limiting beliefs we adopted from abusive experiences should become very clear.

I would like to close this introduction with the following caveat: Although I do not hold the professional credentials of a licensed therapist or counselor and do not have a formal education in psychology, psychiatry, or mental health, I have gone through a journey of healing and have a lifetime of personal experience. I experienced abuse through most of my childhood, I truly suffered from those experiences, and I worked through many difficulties in my adult life to deal with my baggage. I healed and moved beyond my pain, and I vastly improved my life. I believe life experiences can be useful credentials when trying to help others who are journeying through similar challenges. I also know and realize that my journey, course work, and completion of the requirements to become licensed as a professional practitioner vastly helped to place me in a role where I can facilitate others on their healing journeys through similar experiences.

What I have come to realize is I am a unique individual who has a goal in life and the ability to use my gifts and experiences to help others. I experienced trauma in my life in the form of child abuse, but I found true healing by discovering and making a firm dedication to using beneficial spiritual practices. My goal and hope in writing this book is that by sharing my own life experiences of abuse and describing my recovery and healing process, I can help and direct others toward their own healing. I believe I can help others by sharing the knowledge and wisdom I gained and by describing the tools I discovered and implemented in my own life, which resulted in my healing.

I wrote this book for those who share this pain, to help you move beyond abuse and into healing to live a more fulfilled and successful life. Blessings to you all as you read these pages.

Beyond Abuse

Achieve Healing Through Spiritual Practices

PART • ONE

My Life and My Story

AN INTRODUCTION TO PART ONE

As I wrote this book, I focused on presenting the realizations I came to concerning my own healing. Because of this approach, some of the details of my life may seem unclear. To help orient you to my life story, I include here a basic timeline of my life. Names of individuals have been changed, and geographic locations are kept vague to protect the anonymity of those I include in my story.

I was born in 1981 and raised in a small, predominantly blue-collar, industrial town in the Midwest. I have one brother who is sixteen months older than I. Both of us experienced physical and emotional abuse from our parents throughout our childhood and teen years. Emotional repression, physical violence, verbal abuse, shouting, bullying, manipulation, and control were the norm. There was little affirmative praise in my home. Rather there was an abundance of criticism, judgment, and degradation. Nurturing, play, attention, and affection were largely absent from my childhood. As many therapists have told me over the years, I experienced a significant amount of trauma.

I walked away from these experiences with extremely limiting core beliefs about myself, a tremendous amount of resentment, and a significant amount of repressed emotion and pain. I also learned several behaviors and habits from the relationship dynamics I observed in my parents' relationship to each other that did not serve me later in life in my intimate relationships.

I left my hometown as soon as I could to pursue a college education. I knew this was my ticket out and the means to leave all of the abusive experiences behind me. Unfortunately, I still carried all the baggage from those experiences within me. I had little awareness of these things operating as I ventured into my young adult life, and it all created many challenges for me to work through.

I have been married and divorced twice. I have two sons, one from each relationship. I met each of these women in college. I met my second wife, Anna, at the beginning of my freshman year. We became close friends, and I started developing a romantic interest in her at the close of our first year in college together. However, over the following summer she met another man and became involved in a committed romantic relationship before I ever asked her out. We remained friends throughout our time together in college.

I met my first wife, Rebecca, during my sophomore year. We went to separate schools but maintained a long-distance relationship. We were engaged in 2003, moved across the country to the Rocky Mountain region together in 2004 so I could pursue graduate school, and we married in 2005. We moved to the Pacific Northwest in 2007 for my first job, then eventually settled back in the Rocky Mountain region in 2008.

Rebecca and I were in a relationship for thirteen years and married for nine. We had our son, Dillon, in 2010. I have many good memories of our relationship and of her. Unfortunately, we each carried baggage from our pasts, and a lack of self-awareness on both of our parts for how this affected our relationship caused us to slowly drift apart. We separated in 2014, and our divorce was final in 2015. We have each accomplished a lot of healing work and self-assessment since and owned our parts in contributing to the demise of our marriage. We are now friends and maintain a respectful co-parenting relationship for our son.

Anna and I never had contact with each other while I was married to Rebecca. In what seemed a bizarre coincidence, she reached out to me in an email just a few weeks after I announced my intention to divorce Rebecca. Within a couple of months, Anna relocated to the same city I lived in, and we quickly became romantically involved. We found ourselves unexpectedly pregnant with my second son, Michael, after dating for only four months. I married Anna just two months after getting a decree for my first divorce in 2015, and Michael was born two months later.

From early in our relationship, unhealthy dynamics were present. This relationship was characterized by high conflict, and I experienced frequent verbal abuse. Yet I remained in the relationship. Once we discovered we were pregnant, I felt a sense of responsibility to stay in the relationship. The frequency and intensity of conflict between us increased over time, even with us attempting therapy. Ultimately, she became violent with me on two occasions. After the second occasion, I divorced her. We were married for only fifteen months.

During my second marriage, I began attending a church that teaches Science of Mind principles. Learning these principles and experiencing the dynamics of this abusive relationship sparked a major wake-up call for me. I began realizing I was carrying a significant amount of emotional baggage from my abusive experiences as a child that I had never really confronted. I began to understand how this was playing out in my experiences and in my relationships.

Near the end of 2015, I began an intensive practice of meditation, writing, and prayer, aimed at self-exploration and self-realization. These practices and the subsequent realizations led me to write this book. This began a now seven-year healing journey that is ongoing. I have come a long way, and I still have additional healing to do. I have come to realize that this healing journey never ends.

CHAPTER • 1

Honoring the Abuse

One of my earliest, if not *the* earliest memory of my father was traumatic. He owned one of those rubber Halloween masks you would find in a shop like Spencer Gifts at a mall at the time. It was the face of this old, creepy, wrinkled man with crazy white hair that stuck out in all directions. The color of the flesh on the mask was a pale yellowish brown, as if diseased with jaundice. The countenance on the mask, the pattern in the wrinkles, suggested an individual who had been aged by cruelty and hatred.

Until I was four years old, we lived in a trailer park. This memory comes from a time when we lived in a trailer, so I could not have been more than four years old. My mother later explained to me that my father was laid off of work when I was young. While he was unemployed, my mother took up work part time as a nursing assistant, helping to care for someone living near us who was disabled, and my father stayed home providing care to my brother and me. My mother must have been working at the time of this particular memory, because she was not home.

All I recall was my father donning the mask, then proceeding to chase me throughout the trailer while he was roaring and screaming like a monster in a horror movie. I ran into my bedroom, frantically trying to close the door behind me, and crawled under my bed to hide. My father yanked the door open, got down on the floor on all fours, breathing heavily behind the mask, staring at me, then continued screaming at me and grabbing at my arms and legs beneath the bed. I was terrified and remember begging him to take off the mask, while crying and sobbing. When the torture session was over, he finally took off the mask and left the room laughing.

This was not the only time he terrorized me in this way. I have other recollections of similar incidents when I would try to hide beneath the bedcovers, only to feel his presence and hear him breathing heavily like a monster just feet away. Ultimately, he would grab the bedcovers, rip them off of me, and go through his screaming routine. Or he would hold me down beneath the bedcovers and do his thing. I remember constantly trying to find new and different ways or places to hide, hoping I could ultimately change the outcome and the episodes would stop. It never worked.

The feelings of terror and fear during these incidents overwhelmed me. Even as I write this, these memories still elicit a reaction within me; I can feel the adrenaline coursing through my guts as I sit and type this out.

I hated that mask and remember seeing it at times after we later moved into a new house. I always wanted to throw it away, bury it, or burn it, but I was terrified of the potential consequences.

My father exhibited similar behaviors throughout my entire childhood. I have memories of him grabbing my head with both hands, cupping one hand over my nose and mouth, and literally smothering me until I thrashed around violently out of fear of suffocation and death. Many times, he would do this while sitting on me so I couldn't move. He would not release his grip over my nose and mouth until well beyond a state of panic arose within me.

If you have ever experienced a dangerous episode of nearly drowning and just barely making it up to the surface to take a breath of air, then you can relate to the panic that takes you over in the moment. You realize you are in serious trouble, you may drown, and you will do *anything* to get above the water's surface and breathe. I had to experience this sensation over and over again as a child.

Before I was even a teenager, I understood he did this because he wanted to see me panic. There was a period of time when I would just sit calmly while he would cup his hand over my mouth and nose. I would hold my breath and hope if I did not react he would stop and just let go. Unfortunately, he always won. He would wait until my body and reflexes took over once the sensation of suffocation began, and I started fighting and panicking.

Abuse Disguised as Games

I remember my father's "tickle torture" sessions. In his younger days, my father ranged between 220 and 240 pounds, and this was not from being overweight. He was big and muscular from years of manual labor working construction and in a steel mill. I was a late bloomer and was small as a child and teenager. My freshman year in high school, I only weighed ninety pounds and was 4 feet 11 inches. This much larger man would sit on me and tuck my arms beneath his legs. It was impossible for me to throw him off. From this position he would tickle me nonstop, which quite honestly was a good and playful time I enjoyed.

The issue was the other things he would do while I was stuck in this vulnerable position. He always used chewing tobacco—Skoal fine-cut wintergreen flavor. And he would occasionally take a pinch out of his can and force it into my mouth. I remember it burning my lips and gums, and the taste was so horrible, I wanted to vomit. He would also collect odd and gross things from the carpet—like dog hairs, toenails, chunks of dead skin he had picked from callouses off his hands or feet, even dog food—and similarly force these items into my mouth. He would find sweaty, smelly socks or shoes and put them over my mouth and nose, forcing me to breathe in the odors. Or he would pass gas on me and laugh when I gagged over the smell. He was always amused by the reaction he would get out of me: gagging, spitting, and squirming around trying to free myself or avoid whatever it was he was trying to force into my mouth or over my face.

My older brother was a victim of these behaviors also, but he grew much faster and larger in stature than I did. He was somewhat fortunate, and I use this term with sarcasm, that he did not have to endure this nonsense from my father for as long as I did. I remember my father used to hold him tightly beneath a blanket while my brother freaked out in terror trying to escape. Not surprisingly, he grew up with claustrophobia and still carries this fear with him.

There came a day when my brother was able to buck so wildly beneath the blanket he threw my father off, and that was when his torture sessions ceased. Other forms of physical abuse, unfortunately, did not. Those continued for each of us until we moved out of the house as young adults.

My brother and I both have a memory of going to a state park with my parents when we were quite young. There were several views over cliff edges down to waterfalls and the pools below. My brother and I both recall my father holding us by our legs upside down, dangling us over these edges, and lurching us downward with a rapid squat of his hips to give us the sensation we were being dropped. He would do this several times, despite our screams and protests. There was also a creek that ran through our hometown. At one location above the creek on a high bank, there was a concrete bridge abutment from an abandoned railroad grade. My father did the same thing with us over the edge of this concrete abutment with the creek swirling below.

We once had a three-way pillow fight once in my brother's bedroom. I remember my father hit me so hard in the head with a feather pillow, with the feathers packed down into the end of it, my head snapped to the side and hit the wall. I was knocked out cold, unconscious. I probably had a concussion, but it was never treated or diagnosed. And again, this was fun and enjoyment for the man.

Another game our father played involved us boys hiding in the hallway while he sat in his recliner opposite the opening to the hallway. He would throw one of those large super balls (the solid rubber bouncy balls about the size of a baseball) as hard as he could into the hallway. It would ricochet back and forth off the walls, and if we were lucky, we didn't get hit. But if it caught us just right or too early in its trajectory, it left bruises.

We became vulnerable targets when we had to retrieve the ball and venture close enough to the living room to toss it back to him. Then we had to dive for cover before he threw it again with all his might.

He also had a frequent behavior of barging into the bathroom and throwing a bucket of cold water or even ice water on me while I was taking a hot bath. Or he would sneak quietly to the bathroom door and then bang on it suddenly and loudly to frighten me.

All of these activities were his so-called games, all sources of entertainment and amusement to him. It has since become clear to me, he found enjoyment in torturing those smaller and weaker than he was. My brother and I even have memories of him torturing or abusing animals. I witnessed him dozens of times slapping our German Shepherd in the face or kicking or punching him in the ribs. My father's sister owned a cat who my father would torment on a regular basis whenever we visited—pulling his tail, flicking him with his middle finger in the nose or face, chasing him, and attempting to scare him. For quite some time, once I grew up and realized what I had gone through, I perceived my father as a cruel and sadistic bully. I could find no other way to describe or rationalize his behavior.

Abuse Disguised as Discipline

The more severe forms of physical abuse came in the form of discipline. This was not healthy discipline being enacted by a parent who was in control, attempting to provide his children with guidance or setting expectations and boundaries. His discipline most often came while angry or in a rage, with a complete loss of temper and no self-control. The disciplinary measures he used were typically over the top and extremely painful.

My father had impressive skills with woodwork in his younger days. He made a lot of unique and useful items. But he crafted one item I was not so impressed with: a large wooden paddle intricately measured out and cut from a board. He carved it to shape with a handle and sanded the edges down smooth. He must have spent a week or more working on this thing. If my memory serves me, it was about two feet in length and an inch thick, made of dense heavy wood—probably oak. He was not sparing in its use.

There were times I was paddled so excessively I could barely walk or sit down, and this was before I was a teenager. I remember once being beaten to the point I did not have the strength to stand on my own feet without my knees giving out—so he did me the favor of holding me up by my forearm to keep me on my feet so he could continue the beating without bending over.

My brother and I got whipped with a leather belt, too, though not as often. This was reserved for more blatant or severe crimes we committed, and it left raised, painful welts behind.

Most of the time when he lost his temper, he would strike us open handed, extremely hard, right across the face, on the side of the head, or on the back of the head. He did this hard enough at times to make me feel dizzy, and there were a few times I went to school with bruises on my face or lumps on my scalp. When we got older, and likely too big or too old to paddle, he would pick us up by the armpits and slam us against walls and doors throughout the house, striking us repeatedly in the face and head. He broke the doorknob off of our bathroom door with my brother's tailbone. He also broke the doorframe of my brother's bedroom by slamming him through the door in the wrong direction.

All the bedrooms had solid oak sliding closet doors, and I remember one particular instance when my father threw me across my room into those closet doors, breaking both of them off their tracks. I fell into the closet on top of one of the doors, and the other door rotated around and nearly fell on top of me. My father ripped the door out of the way and continued pummeling my head and face with his open hands. This was one of the incidents when I had to go to school with bruises and cuts on my face, and I recall lying about where they came from.

My father was also a control freak, and he wanted things done his way. The consequences were sometimes severe if his expectations were not met. He was a proponent of the clean plate club, and we were forced to eat whatever was served and everything served for any meal, even if we didn't like it. My brother and I both recall being forced to gag down canned beets soaked in white vinegar, nearly vomiting at each bite. We both recall being beaten fairly severely as a means to motivate us to choke down the beets when we took too long to eat them.

We often found crafty ways to secretly dispose of food we did not want to eat: throwing it out the kitchen window beneath the magnolia tree next to the house once our parents left the kitchen; running out to the deck from the door in the back of the kitchen and spitting food out into the yard below;

pretending to go to the bathroom with our mouths stuffed so full we must have looked like hamsters, then spitting it all into the toilet; or burying the food armpit deep into a full trash can. There were other creative methods we came up with as well, like swallowing lima beans like pills so we didn't have to taste them.

The worst memories for me revolve around milk. I had to have a glass of milk every evening with dinner. I hated the taste of milk; it made my stomach hurt and cramp up when I had to drink it, and it made me feel bloated and uncomfortable. Because I hated milk, as a small child I'd naturally leave it sitting until the end of the meal when I was forced to choke it down. By this time of course, it would warm up. And to me, there was nothing more repulsive than warm milk. Many times, if I waited long enough, my parents would leave the room and I could carefully and meticulously dump it down the kitchen sink slowly enough so it did not make a sound.

There were a lot of fights with my father over drinking my milk, but one in particular stands out. My mother was not home, and my father took advantage and tried to force a glass of milk on me at lunchtime, which I did not feel was fair at all. As usual, I saved it until the end, then I did not want to drink it because it had gotten warm and my stomach already hurt. My dad started screaming and cursing at me, and I remember just crying and trying to explain I couldn't drink it because it was warm and my stomach hurt.

He responded by putting the milk in the microwave and heating it up more. He slammed it down on the table in front of me and stood over me brooding, which caused me to just cry even more, and I refused to drink it. He ultimately dumped the glass over my head, threw me to the kitchen floor, and beat the hell out of me, striking me repeatedly in the face and head while I was soaked in hot milk. There are few times in my life I recall feeling as low as this.

Verbal and Emotional Abuse

In addition to the physical abuse, my father engaged in a significant amount of emotional and verbal abuse as well. I can no longer recall specific things said to me as clearly as I can recall some of the incidents of physical violence, but I certainly remember how I felt. I constantly felt like I was a disappointment to the man. I was a "weakling," a "crybaby," or a "pussy." I often felt stupid, like I couldn't do anything right or even satisfactorily. At times, I was called on to help him with some project or other, and if I failed to get the right tool or hold whatever it was he needed to be held in place correctly, he would scream profanity and curse in a rage.

I remember just feeling stupid, hopeless, and also terrified.

There were many times my father and brother would gang up on me, pick on me, and make fun of me until I cried. Then, because I was crying, I got bullied even more, and sometimes even beaten if I tried to fight or talk back. I later learned my brother was being bullied in elementary school between second and eighth grades, in addition to being abused at home. So it is no surprise to me now that he lashed out by picking on me so relentlessly. What was difficult to understand is why my dad chose to join in and why he found amusement in crushing my spirit in this manner.

Unwritten and unspoken policies governed the punishments over crying in my home: I was not permitted to express emotions such as sadness, frustration, or disappointment—and definitely not anger. It became clear to me that men and boys were not supposed to cry. Crying was for the women, the weaklings, and the pussies. Most expressions of emotion I exhibited as a child related to sadness, disappointment, frustration, or anger were punished and beaten out of me. Displays of strong emotion were quickly met by my father's raging temper and by multiple blows to the face and head, or by being tossed about and slammed into walls and doors like a rag doll. Because I was not tough enough or large enough to stand my ground in the physical onslaughts, I was not permitted to disagree or express these emotions.

Abuse from My Mother

I experienced physical abuse at the hands of my mother also, though not nearly to the extent inflicted by my father. My mother would also enforce discipline at times when she lost her self-control and reacted in a state of anger. Similar to my father, she would strike me open handed in the face and head when an incident or behavior of mine triggered or provoked her. Unfortunately, she wore rings, which at times resulted in broken skin and cuts. She would also grab my ears and pull them, so hard at times it felt as if she was going to tear them off. She also grew long fingernails and was not sparing in her use of them to pinch and scratch bare skin.

I do not have memories of these reactions from my mother until I was a teenager, and I know I was a difficult teenager to deal with. I developed anger issues, a quick temper, and—as both of my parents eloquently put it—an attitude. Generally, these physical outbursts from my mother were related to me "having an attitude": talking back, wanting to have the last word, getting defensive, and trying to be right.

Unfortunately, these incidents happened frequently when I was a teen, and I remember growing more and more frustrated and angry every time she struck me in the face. When I was in seventh grade, I punched the solid oak doors of my closet out of frustration after one of these incidents and broke my hand. I received a fair amount of ridicule from my parents, the doctor who set the bones, and my seventh-grade teacher for my temper, the injury, and the cast. The doctor and my teacher, though, didn't know the actual circumstances in my home.

My mother was also verbally and emotionally abusive, but in a much different manner than my father. Her form of emotional abuse was not as blatant or harsh as my father's, but it was certainly present. It took me until I was in my thirties to realize what she had done to me as a child was emotionally abusive. She was rarely supportive, affirming, or uplifting. She was often judgmental and harshly critical of my brother and me. She seemed to emphasize, focus on and reinforce whatever we did that was wrong or not good enough. There was repetitive and continual criticism of our flaws or of behaviors she saw as negative, but little, if any, praise or encouragement.

My brother and I both recall having to clean up the kitchen after dinner every night as children. This was one of our regular and expected chores. It never seemed to matter how thorough or obsessive a job we did, or how convinced we were the kitchen was spotless, our mother would come in and point out and criticize little details she said were wrong or not good enough. I dared not argue with her or protest, because when I did, she would slap me in the face or punish me in some other way.

When I was a teenager, she often projected a negative spin on my behaviors or my words that I felt was not there. There was a major disconnect between my intention in saying or doing something and her perception of the event or of what was spoken. Actions I took that I felt at the time were harmless, questions asked, or statements made were perceived as malicious. She would perceive anger, or this "attitude" as she referred to it, in my tone of voice, when I believed I was completely calm and relaxed. I would then get worked up, trying to defend myself or explain that what she thought she experienced was not true.

I recall experiencing anger, frustration, and, at times, fear and anxiety because of the repetitive patterns that had developed. And I had an expectation of what was coming. Inevitably, her accusations would give rise to emotions in me that were exactly what she perceived as an attitude, which was then met with violence: a sharp open-handed crack square across my face.

Similarly, she projected moods and states of being onto me that I was not actually experiencing. I was often accused of being angry, grumpy, and moody when I was perfectly happy. If I tried to argue this or explain that her assumptions were not true, the incident typically ended in me getting struck in the face. I truly felt at many times she was doing this just for the purpose of starting a fight, to create conflict, and the more I tried to avoid it or just asked to be left alone, the more I got hit.

It is clear to me now that I did not have the ability to communicate my feelings and the things I wanted to say in an effective, respectful manner. It is no surprise, because this skill certainly was not taught or demonstrated to me in my upbringing. Most conflict in my home was resolved by shouting, verbal abuse, and physical violence. So, once provoked, I typically would show up with an attitude and a lot of anger, which resulted in more physical violence. I remember feeling completely frustrated that my voice was not heard, my opinions did not matter, and my feelings and emotions were not important. Essentially, if my parents did not want to listen to me or did not like what they heard from me, they reacted with a quick and violent strike to shut me down and shut me up.

I was taught through violence to suppress my emotions.

Violence Between My Parents

When I was a teenager, violence erupted between my parents on a couple of occasions. They fought frequently and loudly throughout my childhood. I have a lot of memories of my father screaming at the top of his lungs at my mother, cursing and swearing, and assaulting her with verbal abuse. I was awakened one night to the sound of him slapping her, which terrified me so badly I could not sleep the rest of the night.

There was another time when they were fighting, and I heard a slap, then another, and another. My mother started screaming for my brother to help, but he did not wake up.

Adrenaline surged through my body, and I did the only thing I could think of to help: I grabbed a baseball bat from my closet and ran into the living room. My father was holding onto my mother's arm, about to strike her again with his other hand. I shouted as loudly as I could, "GET OFF OF HER! LEAVE HER ALONE!" I knew I did not have it in me to use the bat, though, and I felt a deep dread. If my father called my bluff, I was likely to be hurt badly. Thankfully, he walked over, grabbed the bat out of my hands, threw it to the ground, and stormed out of the house. The next day, the incident was not spoken of nor was it ever addressed. I was sixteen at the time.

A month or two after this incident, my mother confronted me in the kitchen over something she was upset about. I do not remember the topic, but I distinctly remember I did not want to fight about it and asked her to leave me alone. She responded instantly by striking me in the face. What happened next was not something I planned or premeditated; it just happened. I punched her square in the face, hard enough to leave a bruise across her jaw. She proceeded to slap me, shove me, and kick me all the way through the house until she forced me into my room, slammed the door, and demanded I not come out. My father was at work, but I remember in that moment feeling a total sense of despair, fear, and anxiety. I figured he would come home and destroy me, and I spent the entire afternoon creating scenarios in my head of what I believed was coming.

When he did come home, I will never forget the words he said to me: "You have no idea how badly I want to deal with this the old-fashioned way, but you would end up in the hospital, and I would end up in prison."

I wound up getting grounded for the rest of the summer, doing hard manual labor around the house and yard. Meanwhile, my mother told relatives and friends of hers at church about how her younger son punched her. I was constantly ridiculed for my actions, but there was certainly no mention of the history of abuse that led up to the event. I felt an overwhelming sense of shame and disappointment in myself during all of this time.

Insufficient Closure

Thankfully, at this stage of my life, I received an unexpected blessing. I had a close aunt from my father's side who bought a new house where I was permitted to go for several weeks to serve a portion of my sentence of hard labor. The first day I showed up at her home to do some work, she laid into me, asking, "How could you possibly hit your own mother?" I completely broke down in tears and spilled everything. So many memories, stories, events, and experiences from the abuse I endured at home came out all at once in one big, emotional dump.

My parents always had a demand of us; it was one of their mantras: "What goes on in our house stays in our house." We were not permitted to talk about anything with neighbors, friends, or other family members. I broke this rule and talked with my friends my age, but they could not help me. My aunt, however, could. I do not know the details of what, if anything, transpired in conversations between her and my parents after I divulged all of this to her. But after she and I had this talk, my parents began going to counseling.

They took me with them to one session, but I remember feeling confused. I had no idea why I was there. I do not remember anyone explaining to me the purpose of being there or what I was supposed to do or say. I felt uncomfortable. I asked to not have to go again, and my parents honored my request.

For the most part, the violence subsided in my home after my parents began going to counseling, although I have memories of some violent interactions between my brother and my father until my brother finally moved out when he was nineteen. Once he moved out, I either did schoolwork, played soccer, or worked a job so I did not have to be at home. Most of my weekends and other free time I spent with my brother at his new place or at other friends' homes. I was rarely home if I had a chance to be gone.

I knew doing well at school was my ticket out, and I studied hard and always earned straight A's on my report cards. I was so relieved when I could finally go to college and leave it all behind me. I even made arrangements to work summer jobs and internships near my campus so I did not have to return home in the summer months.

CHAPTER • 2

The Need to Feel Our Emotions

I do not write about these events to paint my parents in a bad light or to justify any ill feelings, resentment, or anger toward them. I bear no grudge or ill feelings toward them any longer. I write down these details as a means to recall and feel the emotions associated with these experiences—and to allow you, my reader, the opportunity to recall similar or related events in your own lives.

Based on my experience and on reading and hearing the words from others who have dealt with and worked through similar trauma, I know you cannot heal this type of damage by choosing to forget these experiences or by trying to bury them. You must face the trauma and forgive those who brought it into your life if you are to heal yourself. Facing the trauma involves allowing yourself to feel and understand the emotions associated with it.

Emotional injuries are similar to physical injuries to our body. If we choose to ignore a physical injury and continue engaging in activities that aggravate it, the injury will not heal and will only get worse with time. Emotional trauma requires the same care and attention we should provide to a physical injury. We cannot heal it if we do not allow ourselves to feel it and care for it.

To do this, you must recall and recreate the experiences, events, and memories consciously in your mind. You can do this in a variety of settings and with a number of techniques. Trained therapists and life coaches can certainly help. I specifically chose meditation and writing as the tools to accomplish this work in my own life, and I essentially did the work on my own. I found my own methods, coupled with a variety of techniques I learned in books focused on Science of Mind principles, to be more effective for me than anything I picked up from counseling or therapy sessions in the last several years.

Regardless of the methods you choose, this initial step in the healing process is one of the most difficult. We are hard-wired to suppress and forget these experiences. The last thing our brains and bodies want to do is dig up old memories and replay the experiences in our minds while reliving the emotional charge in our bodies. Doing so results in a full re-enactment of the experiences, putting our minds and bodies in a state of fight or flight and emotional distress. However, this is necessary if you want to reach a state of acceptance, to heal and release the experiences, and to move into a state of forgiveness—a fully necessary part of the healing process, as I discuss in the next chapter. Personally, this process took months of daily meditation and writing practice, and it was certainly difficult and at times highly emotionally charged.

Resisting the emotions, not allowing ourselves to feel them, turning them off, avoiding them, or trying to force ourselves to feel something different—these conscious actions result in the experiences and trauma remaining buried within us. We have to consciously choose to fight against our natural tendency and against the lifelong training that says, "No, I'm not going to allow myself to feel angry/resentful/frustrated/sad about this. I'm not even going to think about it. I'm going to forget this and force myself to be happy. I'm going to think of or do something else to distract me from these uncomfortable feelings, something that will make me happy."

Allowing yourself to feel the emotions of your past experience while bringing in healing and loving energy is what ultimately resolves and removes the pain and trauma. For me, moving through this deeply emotional work resulted in what felt like a huge burden being lifted from me. It helped me remove what felt like a black, cancerous lesion from my heart that seemed to restrict and restrain me. The more I did this work, the lighter and lighter I felt, and the easier it was to understand how and why my parents showed up the way they did. It also became easier to accept these experiences in my life, to take what I needed and wanted from these experiences, and to use it for my own personal growth. Most importantly, it allowed me to forgive my parents and rid myself of the resentment I carried around for years.

I am certain most people who have lived through abusive experiences can relate to and have experienced many, if not all, of the same emotions I went through, so I want to share my own. I am also certain those who suffered abuse still feel these emotions if they replay their memories within their minds or get triggered by a similar event in life.

Compassion is our ability to understand, empathize with, and even feel another's emotional state. I want you, my reader, to know that you have my fullest compassion, and I understand what you feel and what you have been through.

Of the emotions I felt as a child in these abusive experiences, fear dominates. I spent my entire childhood being terrified of my father. The sound of his car or truck pulling up to the curb in front of our house when he returned from work typically elicited a powerful surge of fear and dread within me. I did not want to be near him, and I did not want him to touch me or talk to me. I dreaded most of the times when he would call my name or walk into the same room I was in. I rejoiced at the times when he would call home and my mother would announce he was working a double shift at the mill and would not be home until past our bedtime. I truly enjoyed, and felt great relief, when he worked an evening shift, from 3 p.m. until 11:30 p.m. This meant he was gone before I returned home from school and arrived home after I went to sleep, and he was sleeping too late to see us off in the mornings.

The most intense fear occurred when I was stuck at home alone with my father, without my mother present. This is when his abuse was most rampant. These times were more and more frequent in my later childhood and teen years, as my mother worked an afternoon shift at a grocery store and later enrolled into nursing school.

Fear, therefore, was a constant companion in my childhood. Related to the fear were anger, hatred, frustration, and resentment. All four of these seemed to exist in unison surrounding the abuse and violence in my home. The thought patterns I had as a child and teenager terrify me now, and I still have a hard time believing I harbored these thoughts at such a young age. There were many times after I'd taken a beating, punishment, or verbal abuse, or when my father was degrading my mother in a fight, when I fantasized about his death. I used to wish he would get injured or killed at work. His job was certainly hazardous, and there were stories of men being killed in that steel mill. I wanted my father to be one of the victims. I also wished for him to be killed in a car accident, and I wished I never had to see his truck pull up to the front of our house again.

I also prayed and had fantasies that my mother would divorce him or leave him, and I would never have to see him again, or something else could happen so he would never be a part of my life. I wanted him to be arrested and thrown in prison, but I was too afraid to call the police. The truth is, I did not realize how bad it really was and did not feel I had a case or a reason to call the police. I believed I would just cause trouble for myself if I attempted to go that route. The unfortunate part of being a child in a town or culture in which no one talks about these things is that you grow up knowing nothing else. You believe it is normal and acceptable.

I honestly had no idea I even experienced trauma and an abusive childhood until long after I moved away and began watching other men with their own children—actually showering them with love, sharing healthy playtime, and doting on them with affection. The realization of what I had experienced came full force once I had my first child. More realizations came to me in speaking with counselors and therapists. I had many therapists tell me, plain and simple, I experienced severe trauma as a child. The truth is, my knowledge as a child was too limited to even be aware I was being abused, let alone to know I had the power and ability to call the police and put a stop to it. I truly did not understand that what was occurring was completely wrong and unacceptable. I thought it was normal, and the old phrase now comes to mind: You don't know what you don't know.

There were times when I actually fantasized about playing a part in my father's death. At times after he would emotionally abuse me and torment me, or after an episode of physical abuse, I recall sitting in my room by myself and stewing, ruminating, and fantasizing about severely hurting the man or even killing him. I remember fantasizing about taking a baseball bat or other object and lashing out at him while he slept. I also had fantasies about him coming at me in a physical assault, and me being able to grab a weapon and fight back, beating him or stabbing him to death.

I hoped and prayed I would grow larger and stronger than he was—and I fantasized about pummeling him with my fists in a vengeful rage once I had the physical ability. I remember seeing the trial of the Menendez brothers unfolding in the media during the 1990s and wondering to myself if this was where I might end up. This was all extremely toxic, and I had no awareness whatsoever that I should even question it or look at it. I was completely absorbed in these emotions and thought patterns. And I never talked about this to anyone at that time, and no one was aware I was experiencing any of this internally.

Being raised in the Catholic Church, I transformed these thought patterns and emotions into guilt and shame. I believed I was a sinner, a terrible person, a contributor to Jesus Christ's death on the cross and the beating and abuse he underwent as documented in the New Testament. I believed my thoughts and my emotions were sins, terrible sins, so the guilt and shame poured in.

    I became suicidal when I was sixteen to eighteen years old, which now is not a surprise to me. Fantasies of my father's death turned into fantasies of my own. I wished for car accidents or some other random misfortune to befall me and result in my death. Thankfully, I developed such a fear and dislike of physical pain from my abuse, I did not have the courage to attempt a self-inflicted means to my own death. I now know I was deeply depressed, disturbed, and had not even a shred of emotional health at this time in my life. I had no way and no knowledge of how to express those emotions, and I had no awareness or ability to even look at my own emotional state at that time.

    Over the past several years, in looking back at all of this and doing the healing work, I realized I had picked up and carried a deeply held core belief about myself: that I was no good or that I was a bad person. This core belief manifested in so many different aspects of my life—in truth, in all aspects of my life—for decades. It persisted until I identified it, brought my awareness to all the thought and behavior patterns associated with it, and began working to heal it.

    The truth is, I am not sure if we ever fully heal these things. Residual struggles and triggers frequently seem to pop up. Many individuals much older than I whom I have spoken with and who have been doing this work far longer than I have, indicate it just keeps coming. But they reassured me, and I can also reassure others: It gets easier the more dedicated you are to the spiritual practices we explore in this book and the more you train your mind to self-awareness and being present.

In the course of doing this work, I realized that I carried anger and resentment with me my entire life until I was thirty-four years old. I had been living for thirty years in a state of fear, anger, and resentment. These emotions, and the belief system I subconsciously adopted, affected every aspect of my life during those thirty years, likely beginning from the moment of that initial memory I have of my father and his awful Halloween mask and likely reinforced throughout the rest of my childhood.

CHAPTER • 3

Release the Resentment and Forgive

Up until a couple of years ago, my understanding of forgiveness was fairly shallow, basic, and a bit out of alignment with what the process truly encompasses. My previous understanding of the word or process went something like this:

> Someone does something, either deliberate or unintentional, that results in a painful emotional reaction within me — anger, sadness, frustration, disappointment. I then bring the experience up to the individual, and if I am lucky, they admit to and own the infraction and recognize or acknowledge the pain it caused me. If they do not own the infraction or acknowledge their part in it, they leave me nursing a grudge.

My understanding of forgiveness was limited to someone owning an infraction and responding with an apology. I would then respond, out of politeness or proper etiquette, with the phrase, "I forgive you." In my mind, there was an agreement made at this time that I would forget the infraction and not bring it up again. Nor would I hang it over the individual's head as a way to make them feel guilt or shame. There was also a process involved whereby I would release the emotions associated with the event and not hold onto them—not hold a grudge or harbor anger, resentment, or a desire for revenge.

Of my basic understanding of forgiveness up until my early to mid-30s, this last part was probably the most useful and the most on-target description of the actual healing process that takes place with forgiveness. But until I reached a greater level of maturity, I had a limited understanding of what this actually meant and the work involved to accomplish it.

The former senior minister at Mile Hi Church, Dr. Roger Teel, writes a beautiful piece on forgiveness in his book *This Life Is Joy*. I quote parts of it here because when I first read his words, I experienced an "Aha!" moment. A light came on, and I felt as though I finally got it, I finally understood what this whole forgiveness business was about. I later learned, though, that I didn't fully understand what it meant until I actually went through the process myself and experienced profound healing.

On the subject of forgiveness, Dr. Teel writes:

> *It is not forgetting. Despite that old trite phrase—forgive and forget!—you really can't forget. Everything we have ever experienced is recorded and stored at deep levels of the mind .... A part of you remembers it all.*

> *Forgiving is not condoning. It is not rationalizing that the conflict or hurt was no big deal, or that what someone did was acceptable.... It is changing your relationship with what happened even though it may have been a hurtful or damaging experience.*

Nor is forgiveness getting on your "high horse" and self-righteously absolving someone of something..., as though you are superior.... Genuine forgiveness is not found in this delusion.

Forgiveness is not entering into martyrdom, either. It's not saying "Oh I forgive. Now you can come back into my life and wreak havoc all over again...." No! Many of the lessons in hurtful incidents challenge us to consider how to take better care of ourselves, how to have effective boundaries, how to love ourselves and others fully enough to refuse to allow demeaning or hurtful behaviors.

Finally, forgiveness is seldom a quick fix. It is seldom a one-time experience, especially when it involves the more significant events of our lives. Instead, forgiving is like peeling back the layers of an onion. We bring our hearts to that healing moment of forgiving and make whatever inroads or progress we can.... A good gauge of this is the genuine sense that you now no longer hold onto the wish that the hurtful experience had never happened.... You have transformed your relationship with the experience, you have grown because of it and have fully established it as a gift upon your path.

Forgiveness is one of the highest expressions of self-love. It is loving yourself enough to move out of that stuck place, to get out of that quicksand. It is taking all of the energy devoted to fear and resentment, and channeling it into something that is constructive, life giving, and uplifting. Forgiveness is freeing yourself to get back to the higher agenda of your life—no longer tethered to the past.

I want to expand on some of these principles as they relate to the experiences of abuse and to explain the realizations I made in my own life to move into a state of forgiveness.

Forgiveness Is Not Forgetting

In Chapter 2, I discussed the first principle—forgiveness is not forgetting. We cannot nor should we try to forget abusive experiences or attempt to bury the trauma and emotions associated with them. What inevitably happens when we travel this route is that the emotions come out over and over again with new people and in new circumstances, and we continue to attract experiences to us that will allow us to feel the same emotional response again and again.

The other unfortunate reality of this strategy of trying to forget is most of us who experienced abuse in our lives choose, either deliberately or subconsciously, self-destructive methods to forget the experiences and emotions, to bury the trauma, and to avoid the feelings associated with it all. A typical response is pleasure seeking, which can lead to addiction to drugs, alcohol, sex, gambling, and other forms of temporary adrenaline rushes.

The anger, bitterness, resentment, and desire for revenge I initially held for my father was projected onto new people and circumstances later in my life, without me even being aware of it. What I learned is that while I was carrying resentment from my past, my focus inevitably became drawn to negative circumstances in my current life or to traits I chose to perceive as negative within those I had close relationships with.

This can affect relationships with friends, family, coworkers, romantic partners, spouses, and even children. This self-destructive and self-serving cycle only results in causing more resentment. The longer the emotions persist beneath the surface, the more likely you will find reasons to resent the current experiences and people in your life until you stop trying to forget the experiences and emotions and actually consciously address them and understand where the resentment initially came from.

You consciously address the resentment by allowing yourself to remember–not trying to forget–the abusive experiences and by allowing yourself to feel and be present with the emotions associated with them. By doing this, you discover the root of the resentment so it doesn't grow and spread like a weed into other areas of your life. Discovering the root of the negative emotions also increases your self-awareness and allows a more objective vantage point for your current experiences, so you can evaluate whether or not current feelings of resentment or anger, etc., are warranted or rational.

I have learned to be grateful when I feel resentment now, as it is generally a good signal I am experiencing something that may not be beneficial to my physical health or to my spiritual growth or to my emotional well-being. Repetitive and frequent occurrences of resentment in life can be a sign or a wake-up call that a change must be made or boundaries must be established. The ego part of us is often downplayed, and resentment is certainly born of the ego. However, it is important to remember that the ego's primary role and function is to protect us from pain. It becomes our responsibility then to bring our awareness to these feelings and to evaluate why they are occurring, to determine if they are warranted or rational, and then to make appropriate conscious decisions.

Joseph Grenny with VitalSmarts wrote an article directing readers to evaluate feelings of resentment as cues to make changes. In it, he writes, "You can literally set a watch by the predictable emergence of resentment and your own coinciding sell-out. Upsets begin with sell-outs. And they end with boundaries. You start blaming others for your problems the instant you surrender responsibility for your own needs and preferences."

However, long-term resentment maintained over time presents a different situation and creates a toxic emotional state. I believe I carried resentment primarily aimed at my father for close to thirty years. Either I did not or I was not able to bring my awareness to this fact until I was thirty-two years old, following my first divorce. I certainly did not forget the experiences I had as a child, but when the memories came up, I never allowed myself to feel the emotions associated with these experiences. As a result, my projection of long-held resentment played out in a fairly destructive manner in my first marriage.

I was with Rebecca for thirteen years, and we were married for nine. I cannot say with certainty when it started (possibly from the beginning) but I know in the latter years of our relationship, my attention focused heavily on traits she possessed, behaviors she exhibited, and aspects of our relationship I found to be negative or did not like. I was guilty of setting expectations on the relationship and on her behaviors and emotions that most often were not met. I would feel resentment as a result.

I now realize my focus and devotion of so much attention on the aspects I found to be negative completely poisoned my perception of her and of our relationship. I also realize this behavior directly mirrors the manner in which my mother showed up in much of my life: with an overly attentive focus and an emphasis on the aspects of me, my behaviors, and my actions that she perceived or judged as negative.

Another habit I had was being overly critical and judgmental. Rebecca would accomplish dozens of tasks around our home, but my attention would be drawn to what was not completed or not done well enough or good enough. I would nitpick, nag, and criticize. I was a control freak and wanted things to be done a certain way. The word *why* became a regular and irritating aspect of my conversations with her: Why can't you? Why don't you? Why didn't you? Why did you? Why do you?

I did not realize I was doing this to her. I had no awareness of it, and typically when she would react with a negative emotional response, I would invalidate or suppress her, which was yet another behavior I learned as a child from my parents. My parents suppressed my negative emotions with violence. I now used words to suppress others' emotions that I did not want to hear about or deal with. I often used phrases like, "There is no reason for you to feel this way." "I can't understand why you are angry (or frustrated, or disappointed, or upset, or sad)." And then this would be followed up with denial or defensiveness related to my role in initiating the emotional response.

With time and marriage counseling, I identified four habits and modes of behavior I now know with certainty I picked up from my childhood and brought into our marriage. At the time, I had no idea where these came from or why I showed up in this manner, but I knew I had these habits, and I wanted to change them:

1. A tendency to hone in on the aspects of a person or circumstance I did not like, as my mother had, followed by a pattern of holding onto resentment over that skewed perception.
2. Showing up with constant criticism over what was not good enough or done well enough for my standards, similar to both of my parents.
3. Invalidating and suppressing another's emotional responses that I perceived as negative—anger, sadness, disappointment, frustration—which is what I experienced as a child, with the exception that my responses were suppressed with violence.
4. Trying to control another person's behaviors with the intention of having my expectations met, as my father did, and again, holding onto resentment when this was not achieved.

Early in our marriage, Rebecca became clinically depressed. She came out of it with the help of therapy and antidepressant medications, but she relapsed in later years and also began experiencing an anxiety disorder. She has since communicated to me that some of her own issues and baggage contributed to these conditions. But I know with certainty and I admit that the way I showed up in our relationship was also a contributing factor.

We ended up seeing several therapists over the course of our marriage. With time, I became aware of the bad habits and behaviors I exhibited and the effects they had on her. I worked hard to change and made a practice to eliminate the word *why* from my vocabulary. I stopped nagging and nitpicking at her and the way she did things, and I worked on my controlling behaviors. I also stopped invalidating her emotions, although I had not yet gained the skill of truly being empathetic.

What I was not aware of at the time, and did not or could not work on because of a lack of awareness, was the underlying current of resentment within me. Those emotions persisted, and even when I tried, I could not shift my focus away from aspects of the marriage I found negative or did not like. I felt I was doing a lot of work, but she was not making the changes I wanted or taking the effort to improve the relationship. Ultimately, she told me she did not know if she was ever going to work on our relationship, and I made a decision to end the marriage at that point. It appeared to me she had similarly latched onto a poisoned view of the relationship and of me due to our history and could not or did not want to put forth the effort to improve it. The relationship had decayed beyond repair for both of us, and I ultimately asked for a divorce.

Once I was in a new relationship with my second wife, Anna, a shocking realization came to me after experiencing several episodes of abuse from her. I recognized that my thought patterns, behaviors, and emotions while going through unpleasant experiences with Anna were identical to what I had experienced toward the tail end of my relationship with Rebecca. Yet, this was a completely new and different person, and the circumstances were completely different. I realized these feelings of resentment in this new relationship were mine to address.

Remembering our abusive experiences helps us develop self-awareness about our reactions to triggers in our lives, to events that bring up emotional responses originally related to the abusive experiences. At times when these emotions erupt, they are uninvited and there is a poor understanding with all parties involved of why they showed up so strongly. John Gottman and Joan DeClaire in their book *The Relationship Cure* describe what they call "enduring vulnerabilities," which often pop up and result in conflict within a romantic relationship. Essentially, if the emotions surrounding abuse remain bottled up within and are never expressed, then completely unrelated and apparently mundane circumstances can rub a raw spot and trigger what appears to others to be a completely irrational and unwarranted emotional reaction. But what actually occurs is that something triggers or reminds us of an abusive experience, sometimes without our awareness, and the reaction we have is actually directed at one of those enduring vulnerabilities rather than at the present circumstance.

If we remain unaware of our own enduring vulnerabilities, then essentially we are out in the world or in our relationships acting and reacting unconsciously to triggers from people in our present-day lives. These individuals in turn likely have no understanding of why we are reacting so strongly to something they see as completely benign. Without understanding our vulnerabilities and communicating clearly within our relationships, conflicts and misunderstandings are inevitable.

In his book *The Power of Now*, Eckhart Tolle explains how all of the experiences we perceive in our life as negative are stored within us as the "pain body." If we fail to bring our awareness to our pain bodies, we are going through life reacting to circumstances instead of consciously responding with self-awareness and presence. He later writes something I found to be a fairly dismal reality check, but I knew it to be true in my adult life: Most romantic relationships consist of nothing more than two pain bodies triggering and feeding one another, which is why many romantic relationships are dysfunctional and characterized by repetitive conflict. I believe this is also why our divorce rate is so high in this country. It is not difficult to understand that if someone has no self-awareness of their pain body or enduring vulnerabilities, and if they are repeatedly triggered and react strongly to those triggers, then this would elicit either a defensive or offensive reaction from the other person if they are similarly unconscious and lack self-awareness. Repetitive and dysfunctional conflict is the result. I am confident most people can see this pattern if they look at their own relationships that have been characterized by repetitive conflict or at dysfunctional relationships they have witnessed between others.

Forgiveness Is Not Condoning

When Dr. Teel discusses his second principle—forgiveness is not condoning—he emphasizes the importance of changing our relationship with experiences that were hurtful in our past. He indicates that we are not denying that certain experiences were hurtful or damaging, nor are we condoning actions from others that were harmful to us. Rather, we are shifting our understanding of these experiences from a place of carrying resentment to a place of taking away what gifts we can from these experiences to assist us in our personal and spiritual growth.

Trying to shift my understanding of my abusive experiences was quite difficult, and I found that it was impossible to even attempt this until I was able to remove myself from the experiences of abuse. This process did not really begin until well into my adult life. I do not believe that a child or a teenager has the emotional capacity, life experience, or maturity to change their understanding of abusive experiences while still remaining immersed in an ongoing toxic environment. Based solely on my own experience, I believe adopting a positive attitude or holding onto hope are far more difficult for a child to accomplish when they are in the midst of abusive, high-conflict relationships. If this has been their life story thus far, they know nothing different. For those of us who experienced abuse as children, these steps of changing our understanding of our abusive experiences and trying to see what gifts came to us by living through and healing from these experiences must come much later in life.

Once we have more life experience and come to the realization that what was done to us was traumatic and damaging, we don't have to try to rationalize or make excuses for the abuse. Plain and simple, violence against another person, especially your own child, is wrong, damaging, and harmful. There is no excuse that condones this behavior, and it is important for those who have experienced abuse to accept this and realize that what they were forced to go through was indeed wrong and hurtful.

Changing our understanding of these experiences is quite different, and it requires us to try to understand why we were abused in the first place. I found that trying to understand why I was abused required me to understand what creates an abuser, what an abuser is, and why people become abusers. It is critical to understand we were not abused through any fault or action of our own. We did not deserve it, and it was not our behaviors or our personalities that caused it. The actions and behaviors of an abuser are solely their responsibility and their choice. The recipients of the abuse are not to blame. Ever.

Changing our understanding of our abusive experiences also requires us to shift our understanding of our abusers, and this is a difficult pill to swallow, especially when we are consumed by resentment, anger, disgust, hatred, and fear toward those who inflicted the pain. These feelings are quite natural, rational, and warranted. For a while, I believed I was justified in holding onto a purely negative perception of the abusers in my life. But this choice demands a heavy price, and I found myself forced to answer the question of whether my negative perception of these individuals was the actual truth of who they are.

Trying to understand the truth about these people is what helped me change my understanding of the abusers in my life and shift toward compassion and forgiveness. By truly seeking to understand what they were struggling with, I experienced a shift—from resenting them, feeling anger toward them, and feeling a desire for revenge to actually being able to feel sorry for them, to feel compassion, and to understand why they showed up the way they did. It should be made clear, though, that understanding why they showed up the way they did certainly does not equate to making excuses for, rationalizing, or condoning their behaviors. Rather, this work brings you a better awareness of the state of mind and emotional patterns of the abuser so you can begin to understand why they behaved as they did.

What exactly is an abuser? What makes an abuser? An abuser is an individual who is suffering with their own pain and hurt from their own beliefs and insecurities about themselves, and who deals with this suffering by lashing out at others. Abusers are people who are struggling with shortfalls, limitations, and hurtful experiences in their lives and do not have the awareness, knowledge, or skills to express their pain using means other than creating pain in the lives of others. An abuser essentially projects their own pain and insecurities onto other people as a coping mechanism.

The unfortunate reality is that abusers typically have no awareness whatsoever that this is what they are doing, nor are they aware of why they show up in life in this manner. Jesus Christ is quoted in the New Testament during his crucifixion as stating, "Father, forgive them, for they do not know what they are doing" (Luke 23:34, International Standard Version). This is the truth about abusers. They oftentimes do not possess the awareness of what they are doing or why.

If it is difficult to adopt this viewpoint or, as I believe, this truth about what an abuser is, then I ask a simple question: If an individual profoundly knew and saw themselves as they truly are–a unique expression of God in this universe, with the same attributes and qualities of God (love, light, compassion, wisdom, understanding, intelligence, joy)–would this person be capable of consistently and persistently abusing others, let alone their own child? No, absolutely not. An abuser is someone who is lost, who is asleep, who does not know who and what they truly are. They see themselves primarily as their limitations, insecurities, and painful experiences.

This does not imply an abuser does not have a conscience or a voice within them telling them what they are doing is wrong. It does not imply they do not experience guilt or shame over their actions. It means they have not yet made the choice to awaken to who they truly are, so they have no ability to show up in a different manner. Their lack of awareness typically reinforces their own guilt and shame, adding fuel to their insecurities, resulting in a greater propensity for abusing others.

My high school Spanish teacher posted a phrase on a display board in his classroom: "Saber es poder." The literal translation of the words is, "To know is to be able." The true translation is, "Knowledge is power." Gaining this knowledge and adopting this perception of abusers in your life, of what and who they really are, is powerful. However, this knowledge is not a power to be used to attack an abuser and attempt revenge by pointing out their insecurities and downfalls in demeaning ways. If the abuser has no awareness of their own insecurities (and many of them do not), they will not truly hear you anyway. Rather, you will face denial from them and perhaps an escalation of conflict by attempting to go this route.

Instead, this knowledge is a power you can use to initiate the process of forgiveness within yourself. The realization of who and what an abuser truly is—an individual who is struggling with their own hurt and pain in life, just like you and I do—allows us to experience compassion for them and helps us move toward a state of forgiveness. Change your relationship with the abuser by changing your perception of the abuser, and try to understand who they are and what causes them to behave in the ways they do.

I began to get an understanding of why my parents behaved toward me in the manner they did from listening and truly understanding what their feelings were in relation to details from their own childhoods. My mother grew up in a household where alcoholism, violence, fights, infidelity, abuse, conflict, and even attempted murder were the norm. She shared enough details with me through my life that I can put the pieces together and understand what she struggles with and why she behaved in the manner she did. She related a story to me in which her mother brought her to a bar in a baby carrier, got wasted, left the bar, and forgot the carrier (with my infant mother in it) sitting in a booth. She also shared a story of her mother breaking a wooden spoon over her back in a beating and told me there were frequent and severe beatings of this nature throughout most of her childhood. She witnessed her mother shooting her father in the leg with a pistol, but the intended target had been his genitals. Her father suffered from alcoholism through most of her childhood and was never truly present. She experienced rampant domestic violence, verbal abuse, child abuse, and neglect.

My father's history is not well known to me. The only story I know of that I can see had a traumatic effect on his life had to do with confusion about his own place within his family. His mother became pregnant with him when she was seventeen. The man she was seeing at the time wanted to marry her, but she did not wish to marry him, so they separated. When my father was born, his grandparents took on the responsibility of raising him. He was brought up believing they were his parents, and that his own mother, aunts, and uncles were actually his siblings. When he was fifteen years old, his grandmother apparently got drunk and said something along the lines of, "I'm not your mother, your sister is." My mother tells me one of the few times she saw my father cry was when he relayed this story to her early in their relationship. He told her he never felt or believed that he belonged to a family. I can now see how that belief has played out in his life. However, it is still difficult for me to understand his propensity for violence and the sadistic way he treated us as children. His siblings have indicated to me even with all that happened, they still all grew up in a relatively loving home where violence and abuse were not rampant.

I found when I looked at my own feelings about my abusive childhood and then looked at how I was behaving at times as an adult in ways out of alignment with who I wanted to be, I better understood what my own parents went through. It helped me understand their struggles and challenges, the tough feelings they must have gone through and likely still are going through. It helped me start feeling a sense of compassion for them instead of the anger and resentment I carried for so long. Ultimately, I was able to change my relationship with them and with the abusive experiences, which moved me deeper into a state of forgiveness.

Changing your relationship with or your understanding of an abuser involves shifting your attention and focus away from the negative perceptions you have of the person and choosing to focus on more positive aspects of them. I relate this to something profound I heard Dr. Michelle Medrano, senior minister at Mile Hi Church, say during one of her talks: "Though I may walk in the valley of the shadow of death, I'm not going to pitch a tent and set up camp there." This is important in understanding the link between "forgiveness is not forgetting" and "changing our relationship" with the abusive experience and the abusers.

There was a seventeen-year period, after I finally moved out of my childhood home and began my adult life, during which I held onto a negative perception of my father as an angry, cruel, and sadistic individual. There were times when I was not fully aware I maintained this perception of him, and there were other times when I certainly was. Holding onto this view of the man created obvious tension in our relationship and in almost all of our personal interactions.

Once out of college, I moved fifteen hundred miles across the country, and my parents remained in the town where I grew up. This long-distance relationship meant we only saw each other one or two times a year, generally for a week at a time. There were also phone calls about once a week. My father changed over these seventeen years. He mellowed out. Gone were the quick temper, sadistic tendencies, and violent reactions that characterized my childhood. But I didn't see it because I was completely stuck in my chosen perception of the man based on his past. My perception of him caused me to seek out and focus on his actions, words, or behaviors I felt reinforced my beliefs about him. With this constant tension, it was no surprise most of our visits were characterized by some amount of conflict, disagreement, and at times hurt feelings on both sides.

When I began experiencing verbal abuse and physical violence from my second wife early in our relationship, and I started feeling those familiar patterns of resentment building, this is when I started meditating with the intention of trying to understand where this came from. During these initial meditations I realized I was holding onto a lot of resentment toward my father and why. I've heard it said before that choosing to hold onto resentment is like drinking poison yourself and hoping in some way this will injure your enemy. This is the truth. I realized I had to change my perception of my father, and I also realized my resentment was poisoning me in other areas of my life.

I decided to shift my focus away from all the characteristics I found negative or distasteful about him, most of which were associated with things that occurred in the past. This is not denial or forgetting. Rather, it is shifting the focus away from these things and accepting that, yes, unpleasant circumstances happened, or, yes, I may have "walked in the valley of the shadow of death, but I don't need to pitch a tent and set up camp there."

I began meditating on aspects of my father that I could truly see as positive, on ways in which I actually admired the man, and on valuable life lessons I learned from good examples he set. For me, it is impossible to believe anyone can be 100 percent "bad." I believe there can be and always is something you can look at in another person, no matter how badly they treated you, and find something good about them.

I took this one step further with my father and began writing him letters to this effect, praising him for the ways he showed up in my life as a good man, as a positive example, and pouring light on the aspects of him I found to be positive. There was a tremendous amount of healing in this for me and based on his reactions when he received these letters, there was healing for him as well. I will never forget the overwhelming feeling of peace, love, and healing that washed over me as I wrote my first letter to him with this intention, dropped it in the mailbox, and thought about him reading my letter. I was completely overwhelmed with a deep sense of peace and gratitude, and there was a massive release of something negative within me that I carried for almost two decades. It was extremely emotional, joyful, and one of the most profound spiritual experiences I have ever felt.

I carried that sense of healing and peace with me for days, and it was wonderful. I wrote him many more letters to this effect over a period of several months, and each time I believe I experienced more and more healing. I am now at the point where I can say with honesty that I love the man, I wish no ill will toward him, there is no resentment or anger remaining in me toward him, I fully accept him for how he is in life, I have truly forgiven him, and I have found great healing in this.

In these letters, I told my father he had an incredible work ethic, and I believe the truth of his work ethic is that it came from an intention to take care of his family. There are some people who become slaves to their careers as a means to avoid their families. I am certain my father worked as hard as he did so our lives could be better. He worked most of his life as a rigger at a steel mill. These are workers who specialize in setting up ropes, pulley systems, and cables to lift extremely heavy objects. It was dangerous work. My father suffered his share of injuries from his work, but whenever the mill called him to work overtime, he rarely, if ever, said no.

The money he made paid the bills, put a roof over our heads, put food on the table, and then some. He was able to put my mother through nursing school, which was a lifelong dream she had. He paid for my brother's college tuition out of pocket. And he paid the portion of my tuition and college expenses that scholarships, grants, and student loans did not cover. These commitments constituted a significant financial sacrifice on his part, and probably represented many thousands of hours of hard manual labor in that mill. He sacrificed a lot on our behalf, and I owe the opportunities I had to go to college, spread my wings, and move into a wonderful career I enjoy due to his efforts, generosity, and willingness to work hard to make our lives better.

I also praised him for his green thumb. As long as I can remember, he grew a garden, and he was good at it. I began gardening myself after I bought my first house and quickly became successful at it, owing a lot of my success to skills I learned from him. My brother and I spent a lot of time working with him in the garden, mixing compost, removing insects from plants, pulling weeds, tilling soil, planting, harvesting, and canning. As a child, I viewed a lot of this as tedious work, but now as an adult, I certainly appreciate everything I learned, and it has all helped me produce good harvests from my own gardens.

My dad built an elaborate growing center in his basement with heating pads and lights to start his plants from seed. I remember that of all the vegetable gardens in our neighborhood (and there were many), his always had the fullest, tallest plants and the best harvests. I was grateful to learn these skills from him and grateful he took the time to teach them.

I previously mentioned that he was good with woodwork. He built elaborate pens for three pet rabbits we had as children. He converted an old wooden television frame into a cage with sliding glass doors to house a pet iguana we adopted from a friend. He also built impressive raised beds in our backyard to create more growing space beyond the vegetable garden.

I admired my dad as an outdoorsman. He hunted for a time before my brother and I were born, and he fished for most of our childhood. When my brother and I were old enough, he would take us on several-day trips to the Appalachian Mountains in West Virginia for fishing and sightseeing. I was not adept at fishing when I was a child and honestly did not enjoy it much then. But I certainly enjoy it now and have become an avid fisherman and a hunter. I do not believe I would have taken up these hobbies had he not spent those times with us and planted those seeds. Even though I did not enjoy the fishing and was not good at it during those trips, I still remember developing a deep sense of appreciation for being out in the wilderness, in the woods, and in nature that sticks with me to this day. I find great peace every time I am in nature, and I know that seed was planted by my father.

I have two boys of my own now, and I have witnessed my father being a grandparent. I am most grateful for this. He truly loves those boys, and he shows it authentically. His smiles and laughter at their antics are full of joy and a display of true happiness. He cooks for them, he takes them on rides in a trailer he tows behind his lawn tractor, he reads to them, and he spends other forms of quality time with them. It's a blessing to see him this way and see how he has changed. And it was a blessing to tell him I truly see him this way now.

The change I made in my perception of my mother was not the sudden, profound shift I made with my father. I do not know the reason, but I recognized her growth and saw her change for the better more gradually and consistently. This gradually shifted our relationship into healthier dynamics with time and with many conversations. I made similar choices with her to the ones I made with my father. I wrote heartfelt letters and sent cards at every opportunity: Mother's Day, her birthday, Christmas, and just occasional cards or letters to send love and kindness. Again, this helped shift my focus away from the negative encounters I experienced at her hands, and it helped me change my perception of her and recognize that her good qualities far outnumber the attributes I chose to see as negative.

My mother has always maintained a strong connection to spirituality, her faith, prayer, and her chosen form of spiritual practices. This has been a cornerstone in her life, and I have witnessed how she used all of this to heal from her own trauma, forgive her parents, and work on her shortcomings. I have seen how maintaining her spirituality provides a means for her to live from an uplifted state of grace and acceptance. This trait in her has inspired me in my own spiritual growth and in my dedication to my practices.

She is generous with her time and energy. She is consistently willing to be an understanding and compassionate presence or to help in some way when she comes across people who are in need, either experiencing emotional distress or a challenging life experience.

Overall, even with the shortcomings I have seen and the ways she hurt me over the years, I can still see that she strives to be a good person and a beneficial presence in the world. I would describe her as a kind, caring, and loving person.

I changed the perception I carried of both of my parents. I made a conscious choice to shift my focus to what I found to be good in them. And I also made a choice to try to understand their emotions related to their own traumatic experiences. This changed my understanding of the abusive experiences I lived through with them, and it changed my relationship with both of them for the better. This was a big step in achieving a state of forgiveness.

Forgiveness Is Not Getting on a High Horse

Dr. Teel's third principle on forgiveness—it is not "getting on your high horse"—is a principle that needs to be kept in mind once we wake up and want to break the cycle of abuse. We know abuse can be generational, with children from abusive homes often following the patterns they learned from their parents and putting their own children through similar painful experiences. This pattern typically persists through many generations, until someone wakes up and makes a change.

Once you wake up and make a conscious choice to behave in a different manner than those who abused you, you may not be well served by pushing your abusers out of your life completely while holding onto the perception that you are now superior to them. Waking up and realizing you show up much differently in your own life and with your own children does not give you a reason or an excuse to look down your nose at those who abused you. Adopting the view that you are now somehow better than those who abused you is nothing more than a different form of resentment. It is an indication that healing has not occurred, and carrying such an attitude within you is the same as carrying resentment. It is poison, and it will transfer onto other people and into other experiences in your life.

I realized this truth related to my relationship with my mother. I previously mentioned that she had a tendency to focus on characteristics or behaviors of mine that she found to be negative. This tendency continued into my early adult life. One of the things she habitually criticized was how I raise my children. I reacted strongly when she chose to provide unwanted advice or just plain criticism about my abilities as a father. Given my experiences as a child at her hands and my father's, the temptation in the past would arise to call her out as a judgmental hypocrite. There were times when my mind would stew with a desire to tell her she had no right to give me advice on how to raise my boys, given what she and my father put me through as a child. When this dynamic was present between us, I wanted to rub her face in her past, and this came from a self-righteous attitude I carried, believing that I had become a far better parent than the ones I had.

The difficulty in this circumstance is recognizing what is truth and what is healthy versus what is an unhealthy or toxic mode of thinking. What I ultimately realized is there was nothing wrong with acknowledging that my mother was, at times, critical and held a negative perception of me. It is certainly beneficial to me and my children that I choose to show up as a father in a way I know is loving, caring, compassionate, engaged, affectionate, and attentive. It was healthy for me to place boundaries and to communicate to my mother (or anyone else) that I will not tolerate unwarranted criticism or verbal assaults about my abilities as a father.

I realized my thoughts were characterized by unhealthy resentment when I wanted to draw comparisons between how I raise my own children versus how my parents raised me. Thinking I am somehow better than my parents were and wanting to point out their mistakes or flaws were resentful thinking patterns. I realized these were defensive reactions that arose within me when my own limitations or negative beliefs about myself were triggered. If I perceived an unjust attack, these strategies came out to deflect the attack and attack in return.

What I have learned to do instead is to accept and know who I am as a father, communicate my boundaries to people who criticize my parenting, and make my best effort not to move into a defensive mode. Knowing who I am and how I behave as a father is enough to ensure I continue showing up for my children in the best way I can. There does not need to be any comparison to others and offering such a comparison certainly does not help me show up better for my boys.

I had to make a choice to see that although my mother criticized me, or that I may have perceived it that way, her intention may not have been to hurt me. Choosing to believe that her intention was to help me help my boys, choosing a different way of perceiving her, and also making the choice to communicate my boundaries quickly defused my defensive reactions.

Dr. Teel's statement, "Forgiveness is not entering into martyrdom," and his discussion of the lessons to take better care of ourselves and to have effective boundaries are critical when it comes to healing from abusive experiences and moving toward forgiveness. It is extremely difficult, if not impossible, to move into a state of forgiveness toward abusers if we continue to experience abuse at their hands or at the hands of another. This underscores the importance of establishing healthy boundaries in our relationships for our own self-care and self-love.

CHAPTER • 4

Setting and Maintaining Healthy Boundaries

As Dr. Teel discusses in his book, forgiveness does not imply becoming a martyr and does not equate to allowing ourselves to be subjected to the same hurtful experiences over and over again. We must set and maintain healthy boundaries in our lives to assist in our healing process. Removing ourselves from abusive experiences and removing abusive individuals from our lives, I believe, is essential before we can begin a forgiveness process.

Boundaries are a personal choice, and each relationship is unique. Similarly, the experiences of the abused and their abusers are widely varied, each unique to those involved. I believe abuse can be defined succinctly as a refusal to respect another person's boundaries. The only advice I offer on what specific boundaries or limits are appropriate for anyone is this: If you suffer abuse from individuals with whom you maintain relationships, the abuse must stop. The only way to stop it is by establishing boundaries and by making agreements with ourselves about what actions we will take in our relationships when our boundaries are not respected.

What I discovered in my life is that my boundaries were poorly defined or, in some cases, nonexistent. For those of us who lived in an abusive environment from our earliest memories, we can have difficulty embracing the concept that we can tell people "no" or "stop." We were not brought up in an environment where our emotions, thoughts, opinions, and needs could be freely or safely expressed. We were not provided with appropriate reinforcement that we have a say in how we are treated, how we are spoken to, or that we deserve respect. We were probably not listened to most times we attempted to express any of these things, or we were met with abusive reactions.

Many of us also adopted habits of seeking approval or attention from those whose love we sought, which may have resulted in a strong fear of rejection or abandonment if we speak up about our boundaries. We become afraid to rock the boat within our relationships based on reactions we became accustomed to from our pasts, and we end up sacrificing far too much of ourselves to maintain a relationship and avoid the potential sting of loneliness, rejection, or abandonment.

The ideas that we matter, that we have a voice, and that we have a need to be listened to and treated with respect can seem quite foreign to us. Attempting to define our boundaries, then learning how to communicate and establish them, can be a bit clumsy at first.

The first step in establishing healthy boundaries is coming to a realization within ourselves that we matter, that we are important, that we are to be loved, cared for, and treated with kindness and respect. Once we arrive at this realization and maintain this belief in ourselves, we then have to go about the business of treating ourselves in this manner through self-love, self-care, self-forgiveness, and by being kind and compassionate with ourselves. If we are stuck in a habit of entertaining self-defeating and sabotaging thoughts, if we constantly criticize and judge ourselves, or if we neglect and physically abuse ourselves, more than likely we are attracting people into our experience and maintaining relationships with those who will reinforce these beliefs and engage in similar behaviors toward us.

Once we start arriving at a place of self-love, self-care, and a realization that we matter, we are then better equipped to start evaluating where boundaries are needed in our relationships. Maintaining those boundaries may come in the form of cooperative, respectful communication and understanding between two people with agreements about actions for positive change. Or establishing such boundaries may involve the complete dissolution of a relationship. Of course, there are infinite options and alternatives between these two scenarios.

The ultimate outcome depends on what you desire for your life, what your goals are for your relationships, what behaviors you are willing to accept from another person, your own emotional health and well-being, the willingness or ability of the other party in the relationship to respect boundaries, and many other variables that are dynamic and constantly changing with time.

If this is new territory, it may be difficult to know where to begin when it comes to defining boundaries. I believe it is necessary to take time, reflect, and write agreements with yourself for those absolute, nonnegotiable, and uncompromising boundaries you want in your relationships. Defining your boundaries includes identifying the behaviors you absolutely will not tolerate from another individual, ways of being treated that you know do not serve you spiritually or emotionally, and words or ways of being spoken to that you will not listen to any longer. Then you must do the work of communicating to individuals with whom you are in relationships what those boundaries are, how you expect them to be respected, and what actions you will take if they are not.

I believe it is important to be firm, to be direct, and to be true to yourself and honor the contract you made with yourself. At the same time, it is important to learn how to communicate these things with other individuals in a way that is kind and respectful. I found that setting boundaries for myself and communicating them to others, especially when this was outside the established pattern or dynamic in the relationship, could be quite difficult. However, it was absolutely necessary for my healing. This must be seen as a step toward your own self-love and self-care, and as a blessing and a gift to yourself to build your life and relationships in a more positive environment.

Once we begin a process of waking up to who we really are, we may be a bit surprised when we start taking a look at our relationships, the types of people we have attracted into our experience, and the dynamics we maintain with them.

A New Relationship

Following my first divorce, I quickly engaged in a new relationship with another woman who I knew from earlier in my life, Anna. I began experiencing verbal and emotional abuse from her very early in this relationship, and these dynamics quickly became a repetitive pattern. There were red flags and warnings early on, and I disregarded them. I discovered the reasons for this after I woke up a bit, which I will discuss after I share a bit of this story.

Anna and I lost contact with one another once I moved across the country and married Rebecca. However, about three years before Rebecca and I divorced, I suddenly began having recurring dreams about Anna, many of which had a romantic component to them. These dreams continued off and on every few months for about three years, and I did not understand why I was having them, nor did I pay them much attention. When I began considering a divorce from Rebecca, a close friend of mine asked me if I would ever remarry. When he asked this, I thought about these dreams I had about Anna over the past several years, and I told him that if Anna ever showed up in my life again and was single, I would consider pursuing a relationship of that nature with her.

It was approximately 18 months after I had this conversation with him when one of the most bizarre experiences occurred that I had ever encountered. Six weeks after I told Rebecca I wanted a divorce, I received an email from Anna, completely unexpectedly after nine years without contact. She wrote that she was traveling to the city where I lived and hoped for a visit with me. She was considering that city for a permanent move, seeking a change and new employment opportunities. I was in such a state of shock after receiving this email. The way this was unfolding was identical to the dreams I had while we were not in contact with each other. I remember having to stop what I was doing and actually sit down to collect myself. I could not believe it. This seemed like one of those things that happens in movies, or in fairy tales, or that you hear about happening to other people. I never expect something like this to happen to me.

Anna was also single at this time, having recently ended a romantic relationship. She visited for a few days, and we spent quite a bit of time together. We discovered we still had a lot in common: similar values, life goals, spiritual beliefs, and hobbies. We had even been reading a lot of the same books on philosophy, relationships, and spirituality over the nine years we were not in contact. After that visit, we talked on the phone and emailed one another regularly. In one of these conversations, she shared with me that she had told a friend years ago that she wished she had married her best friend from college, leaving me once again shocked by the synchronicity.

She decided to relocate within a couple of months after initiating that first contact. Once she moved, we quickly became romantically involved. At the time, it felt like I was in a fairy tale —she was the "one who got away." It felt like it was meant to be and literally like a dream come true.

We found ourselves unexpectedly pregnant after dating for only four months. We decided to marry before our son, Michael, was born. But, the marriage only lasted for fifteen months.

How I Attracted this Relationship

I was unfamiliar with the principles of Science of Mind when I was married to Anna, but I now realize that this experience was meant to be, but not for the reasons or fantasies I attached to it. I am now convinced that reconnecting with Anna at this particular time was related to the resentment I carried within me and projected for years prior to her reappearance in my life. Dr. Joe Dispenza summarizes this concept in his book, *Breaking the Habit of Being Yourself*. He discusses that if we experience a particular emotion regularly and hold that emotion in our thoughts, feelings, and behaviors, we broadcast a powerful signal into a Universal Field of Intelligence that responds by manifesting experiences that produce the same intellectual and emotional responses.

This is one of the fundamental principles taught in the Science of Mind philosophy. I believe the energy I broadcasted all of those years toward my parents and Rebecca resulted in me inviting another new experience that allowed me to experience additional resentment.

I also now understand that I operated at this time in my life with little awareness of what my needs and boundaries were within an intimate, romantic partnership. This relationship with Anna served as a significant wake-up call to me that I needed to get clear about my boundaries and get clear about what decisions or actions I need to take if they are not being respected. Essentially, I operated at this time with the same level of awareness I operated with as a child. I had little understanding of what a boundary even was for me within the confines of this type of relationship. I did not have any well-defined boundaries for myself, and I certainly was not in a place to be able to communicate these things effectively.

The Relationship Dynamics

To be fair, Anna is a good woman at heart. As long as I have known her, she has always been responsible in her life. She is one of the most intelligent individuals I have met, and she has succeeded in achieving her career goals using her intellect and ambition. I saw her make real efforts to be kind, caring, and compassionate toward others. I appreciated her sense of humor, and we shared a lot of positive experiences and memories together. When things were peaceful, we enjoyed our time together. This is the positive side to why I tried to remain in the relationship with her for as long as I did.

To be realistic, honest, and inclusive of the whole picture though, I also have to describe the unpleasant characteristics she displayed that affected our relationship. Early in our relationship, she emailed me, sharing that she had a fear of abandonment due to trauma from her childhood. She also shared with me that she carried a limiting core belief that she was unlovable.

She understood that these issues caused her to behave in ways within her romantic relationships that reinforced her fears and beliefs. What I did not realize was the severe level to which she would escalate in her attempts to push me away—whether consciously or subconsciously, I may never know. Despite her awareness of these things operating within her, she had little or no control over her emotions and reactions when these fears or beliefs were triggered.

Our relationship suffered from repetitive conflict for its entire duration. Both of us moved easily and quickly into a triggered state with one another, and, as a result, disagreements quickly escalated to high conflict. Anna struggled with trust issues and maintained that I would either cheat on her or resume a romantic involvement with Rebecca. She brought these concerns up in ways that came across as accusatory. I also experienced a recurring pattern in which sensitive or vulnerable information I previously shared with her would be turned against me and used as weapons, and the things she brought up often were not related to the disagreement at hand. To these and other accusations she made, I most often reacted with defensiveness.

I found Anna also to be quite defensive, likely in response to a level of harshness or forcefulness I used in bringing up my own concerns to her. What I thought at the time were harmless suggestions, questions, or inquiries were interpreted by her as attacks; and she often responded by attacking in return. In this manner, we would lock horns, and disagreements were never resolved, nor were they handled in a healthy manner by either of us. Shouting, profanity, blaming, and name-calling became the norm between us.

There was one firm boundary I defined for myself, which I considered a nonnegotiable deal breaker. That boundary was no physical contact or violence to be used when either of us was in a state of anger or engaged in conflict with each other. Anna crossed this boundary for the first time when a long-standing disagreement over our son blew up into a shouting match and she eventually slapped me and shoved me. Yet even with this boundary being defined for me as a deal breaker, I did not leave or end the relationship when it happened.

Instead, our relationship continued for an additional ten months following this incident, with no change to the level of conflict we were both experiencing and engaging in. Throughout all of this, I struggled with feelings of resentment and uncertainty about what to do. We were seeing our second marriage counselor, and I hoped and prayed the counseling would work and things would calm down. I wanted the relationship to work, because I struggled with the idea of putting my older son through another divorce so soon after he had just experienced one. Ultimately, the decision was made for me, as my nonnegotiable boundary of no violence in the home was crossed a second time. I chose to divorce her at this time, and we both engaged in a high-conflict divorce process that turned into a significant financial hardship for me.

Similar to my first chapter where I describe the abuse I experienced from my parents, I do not share the dynamics or some of the details of my relationship with Anna while holding an intention to embarrass her. My hope is my readers can understand and relate to circumstances in their own lives where they have remained in a toxic situation out of either fear or an inability to communicate and honor their own boundaries. I am aware some lessons in life come in the form of trauma, and this was one of those lessons for me. It is difficult for me to describe the profound impact these experiences had on me without also sharing some of the details of the trauma I experienced. I recognize now that both Anna and I were traumatizing one another in how we each showed up in this relationship.

I remained in this relationship with Anna for nearly two-and-a-half years, and the dynamics of conflict I describe were prevalent through the duration of our time together. Once it ended, I was left asking myself why I remained engaged in this situation for so long if it was this volatile and unpleasant. I observed warning signs early in our relationship, but I disregarded them. Why did I allow myself to continue experiencing these dynamics? Why did I allow myself to be treated this way, and why did I act in the ways that I had? Why didn't I end the relationship before it escalated to the level of violence? Answering these questions is what led me to wake up, and resulted in the realizations that started me on my healing journey.

My Wake-up Call for the Need to Set Healthy Boundaries

I came to the realization that I did not know how to set or maintain boundaries for myself in any of my relationships. In particular, I realized defining and communicating my boundaries within the setting of a romantic relationship was quite difficult for me. The only real boundary I had was that I would not tolerate violence in my home. It is clear to me now that I needed to define and maintain many others in regards to how I wanted to be treated and to establish the healthier dynamics I wished to be present. I also realized a need to establish boundaries for myself and for my own behavior as to how I would respond or show up in moments when I became triggered so that I would no longer engage in high levels of conflict.

I realized my choices to disregard unhealthy dynamics were driven by my limiting subconscious beliefs that I was no good or not a good person. Essentially, I believed I could not attract a better partner or that I did not deserve any better. My self-worth and self-value depended on whether or not I won the attention or affection of a woman, even one who treated me poorly.

I have learned it is common for individuals who have experienced abuse at the hands of their parents to subconsciously seek out abusive or neglectful relationships and to participate in abusive dynamics. I also realized I struggled with an addiction to sex and romantic relationships.

In addition to learning that I had poorly defined boundaries, I further learned through this relationship that I did not have the ability to calmly and respectfully communicate my boundaries in a way that was kind both to myself and to another. What I found myself doing instead was engaging in those behaviors I was familiar with, those behaviors I learned from my parents growing up, and those coping mechanisms I used in my youth to deal with emotional pain.

I did not have an ability to communicate how it felt to have my integrity and my commitment repeatedly questioned. I was unable to express the pain I felt when Anna condemned me over experiences from my past that I had not yet healed. I was unable to calmly communicate my intentions to provide the best care I was capable of to our son. I did not have the ability to respectfully or calmly say, "No," or "Stop," in a way that was kind and compassionate to myself or to her.

What I did know how to do was react to her in an extremely defensive manner. I knew how to fight back and assert myself, and I knew how to argue in a way to make myself feel right. I knew how to scream when I was being screamed at and how to use profanity against her when it was being used against me. I knew how to attack her in kind, point out her flaws and vulnerabilities and the ways they revealed themselves in our relationship. I never got violent with her, but I certainly knew how to be abusive with my words in return. None of it was productive, and it was a waste of energy. It only hurt me, her, and others who witnessed these dynamics between us.

We are better served by defining healthy boundaries and learning how to communicate them in a way that is calm, kind, and respectful. We have to realize and own that we likely do not have the ability to do this in the midst of a conflict. We need to learn to disengage, walk away, calm ourselves down, and talk in a way that expresses how we feel, rather than bringing up accusations of how the other party is behaving—in other words, using "I feel" statements instead of "you" statements. If we witness the other party being unwilling to listen to us or unable to respect our boundaries, then we have to be brave enough to change the dynamics of the relationship to care for ourselves. Within the settings of an intimate, romantic relationship, we may have to be brave enough to end the relationship and walk away.

My Forgiveness Process with Anna

Forgiving Anna was a much different process than what I experienced in forgiving my mother and father. I realized every relationship is unique; every individual is unique. Therefore, every experience of forgiveness we encounter in our lives is going to have its own unique processes and characteristics. All that is required of us is to be open to forgiveness, and we then allow the processing, the thoughts, the emotions, and the realizations to come to us in time. We have to allow this process to happen on its own; it cannot be forced or bypassed. If you find yourself stuck or not knowing where to begin, even if you carry an intention to forgive others from your past, you can find assistance through therapists or counselors and find useful techniques to work through forgiveness in spiritual books, classes, or workshops.

For me, a significant step in achieving a state of forgiveness was to own my part and to forgive myself. I understood how I contributed to the conflict we experienced with my own defensive reactions. I realized my failures to communicate and honor my own boundaries, and I identified the reasons behind my behaviors. I also realized I was engaged in a significant power struggle with Anna, and most of the fighting on my part was aimed at getting her to change, instead of just accepting her as she was. I have since learned that we can love and accept someone exactly as they are, but doing so does not necessitate remaining in a close or intimate relationship with them.

Another piece I found necessary in this forgiveness process was releasing the resentment I held for her and owning how that resentment affected my life and our interactions. Holding onto this resentment kept me engaged in conflict with her for almost two years following our separation and divorce. I ultimately realized it was being fueled by a desire to get her to change how she treated me, which was no different than the power struggle I engaged in with her while we were married. I had to let go of this desire, and I came to the realization that I cannot force her—or anyone—to change. I understood that I must allow her to come into her awareness and healing in her own time and in her own manner. I had to accept it is not my responsibility to teach her or anyone else their lessons.

I found I was unable to write about all of this in a way that was fair to either of us until I released my resentment toward her. Once I processed this and completely let go of the desire to change her, forgiveness for her gradually took over. I am in a place now where I truly wish her nothing but happiness and joy. I believe I understand why she behaved the way she did in our relationship, and I have found compassion for her through doing my own inner work. This understanding and compassion helps me respond to her with respect and kindness, while still remaining firm in my boundaries with her.

Most importantly for me, I have come to a place where the ways she chooses to treat me no longer have any effect on me. This entire experience proved to me that you cannot achieve forgiveness for another individual or begin any healing process for yourself if you are maintaining an abusive relationship with that person.

The Need for Boundaries in All Our Relationships

Anna provided me with an additional gift from our experiences with one another. I came away with the realization that not only did I neglect to establish boundaries within my romantic relationships, but I also maintained the same habit in most of my other relationships. This became apparent for me in my adult relationship with my mother. Shortly after Anna and I separated, I became aware of many dynamics present in my relationship with my mother that were identical to experiences I had with Anna. I was alarmed to discover this, but again, it was necessary for my own healing and growth. I was not aware nor did I have any recollection that my mother emotionally abused me as a child. This process of awakening helped me recognize several unhealthy dynamics between my mother and me, and this realization came to me in a fairly unique manner.

Several toxic patterns between my mother and me surfaced through vivid and recurring dreams that persisted over a period of nearly eight months following my separation with Anna. My grandmother passed away the day after I told Anna I wanted a divorce. A couple of months after she passed away, she came to me in the first of these dreams. It was clear to me that she was communicating an unhealthy dynamic that existed between my mother and me, so I could do my part to heal myself. This dream brought to my awareness my mother's pattern of regularly being critical of me and my role in reacting defensively.

Over the next several months, I had recurring nightmares of conflict with my mother. Many of these conflicts were extremely violent, and there was a lot of strong emotion in these dreams.

I typically visited my hometown with my boys each year, as we still do, to see my parents and extended family. I took one of these trips in July 2017, and it was the same as any other since I moved across the country as an adult, with my mother and I getting into a major conflict. This seemed to be the norm nearly every time my parents came across the country to visit with me and their grandchildren or when I returned to their home to visit with them.

This time in 2017, however, I had the gift of my full self-awareness and presence and did not react or engage with her. I was able to sit back, completely disengage, and observe her without any judgment. I was able to see clearly what she was doing, how she was showing up, and how she was acting toward me. I realized she was stuck in the mode of creating conflict that had persisted since I was a child by projecting emotions onto me, while being critical and judgmental.

During this visit, I also became aware that there was a significant disconnect between my intentions behind something I did or said and my mother's perception of the event—similar to what existed in my relationship with Anna. I had to own the harshness I used when bringing up concerns to my mother, and I also had to realize that she has a tendency to react defensively when she feels criticized.

These patterns were on full display during this visit. For the first time in my life, though, I did not get defensive or engage with her. However, my avoidance of conflict with her and my refusal to react were not enough to diffuse the situation. Over the course of my visit, her behaviors and reactions became more and more volatile, and it got to a point where she began directing false accusations toward me about being disrespectful and showing up with anger; while I knew I was in a space of complete self-control, being calm, and remaining quiet. Her speech toward me eventually ramped up to criticizing how I raise my children. She also began insulting the church I go to, my faith, and my spiritual practices. I responded to her criticisms calmly, and stated I was not going to engage in conversations with her on these topics.

This resulted in a more violent reaction from my mother. She began shouting and using profanity. I still remained calm, and I listened to her as she projected her emotions onto me, stating that I was the one raising my voice and getting disrespectful in the conversation, that I was the one who was angry. A moment occurred when I saw a flash of anger in her eyes and face, and I thought for sure she was about to hit me. It immediately brought back memories from my childhood. I stated very clearly to her that if this was how she chose to engage with and talk to me, then the conversation was over. I told her I was not going to allow her to speak to me in this manner, with criticism, accusations, shouting, and profanity. I left the house and spent the remainder of the trip with my brother.

Over the next several months, I was able to go back into my memories of previous visits with my parents during my adult years. I was able to clearly identify these same patterns and the conflicts that would escalate due, in part, to my defensive reactions. I was able to recall past phone conversations when my mother exhibited these same behaviors toward me, and I observed her doing so in phone conversations following this visit as well. I realized that many of the behaviors and tendencies my mother showed during my childhood still persisted to this day—though without the previous physical violence. The criticism and judgment simply took on different forms and new topics.

The most common theme of her criticism was over how I raise my boys. During most visits my parents made across the country to visit us, I was met with repetitive questions from my mother regarding many of my decisions or actions in taking care of my children, always beginning with, "Why are you…? Why did you…? Why don't you…?" These criticisms came forth in nearly every aspect of how I raised my children: how I let them play, their diets and eating habits, their hygiene, their nap times and bedtimes, how I chose to discipline them, the responsibilities or chores I assigned them, and the level of freedom I let them operate with. It did not matter what I was doing, she continually offered criticism and questioned my decisions. There were several times she became quite abusive with her language.

I began seeing that my role in these conflicts was to react defensively, similar to how I had when I experienced abuse from Anna during our marriage. I also had a sinking realization that Anna and my mother were similar in some ways and shared many common behaviors. I realized I may have sought out a relationship with a woman who felt familiar to me.

Over the next couple of months following that 2017 visit and during phone conversations in which the same behaviors occurred, I began attempting to discuss my observations with my mother in a respectful manner. I also tried to explain how I felt about these behaviors. I realized I needed to establish some boundaries in how she interacted with me, but it soon became clear to me that it was hopeless to attempt this in a face-to-face conversation or over the phone. She would start shouting, or she denied plain facts, interrupted me mid sentence, changed the subject, and refused to listen when I tried to explain my feelings. This was incredibly frustrating. I soon realized this was another behavior she had engaged in since my childhood—interrupting, using verbal violence, and shouting as a means to shut me up and shut me down if I wished to communicate my thoughts or feelings over some experience or circumstance that she did not want to discuss.

Ultimately, I decided to write her a letter. It was the only way I knew to get what I wanted to say out and to communicate my feelings without being interrupted or invalidated. It took me more than three hours to write it, and I sat on it for two days, reading and rereading it before I decided to send it.

I kept the letter factual and respectful, describing the dynamics I saw between us, the ways in which I was being spoken to and treated, the criticism I experienced on a regular basis. And I provided many examples. I admitted to my roles in these conflicts and discussed the deep work I was doing on myself to address my part. I made a commitment to continue doing that inner work for the sake of our relationship. I also communicated clearly how this all made me feel.

I closed the letter with specific boundaries that I intended to maintain in our interactions moving forward: I would not tolerate shouting, profanity, projection of emotions, abusive criticism or accusations, judgment of how I raise my kids, or judgment over my choices in my romantic relationships, friendships, church, faith, or spiritual practices.

The day I sent that letter to her, the recurring nightmares over conflict and violence between us ceased and never returned.

My mother did not write back or speak to me for more than two months. Then one day, she called and asked to talk. She offered an authentic and sincere apology to me, but she also communicated that she did not actually read my letter. The following year when I returned home for another visit, these behaviors erupted again. The same patterns of projecting emotional states onto me, criticizing my parenting, and not allowing me to speak about my thoughts or feelings continued. I wrote another letter to both of my parents, essentially communicating the same information for a second time. This time, I made it clear that I would not be returning to their home or inviting them to my home unless these behaviors and patterns changed or unless they chose to listen to me.

Once again, many months went by without any communication from either of them. Eventually, my mother called to inform me that once again she refused to read my letter.

My response to her was simple: If one party in a relationship refuses to listen to the thoughts or feelings of another and refuses to listen to or respect their boundaries, then there can be no relationship. I indicated that I would no longer try to maintain a relationship with either of my parents if this dynamic persisted. I was able to maintain my insistence on this without experiencing any guilt or shame, because I knew I had done this in a way that was kind, loving, and respectful.

It took my parents nearly a year before they finally read my letter, and began reestablishing communication with me. During this strained time in our relationship, all of us had a desire to move forward with each other in a more respectful manner. It was clumsy and awkward for all of us initially. What was most important to me was that my parents were willing to listen to me and hear me out. This was a major shift from my prior experiences with them. After many conversations around how we all wished to be treated, then after apologies and agreements, we have all been able to create much healthier relationships with one another.

These experiences taught me that setting and maintaining healthy boundaries is a completely necessary practice for achieving a state of forgiveness and also necessary in healing from abusive experiences. They also taught me that we cannot set expectations for another party in a relationship to respect our boundaries. Rather, we must do what is necessary for our own self-love and self-care, even if this means drastically changing or ending relationships with spouses or parents.

Finally, I learned the importance in our forgiveness work of owning our own mistakes and how we may have violated someone else's boundaries. Healing and true forgiveness does not occur without this necessary step.

What I can say with certainty is that I am so grateful I learned how to set and maintain my own boundaries, and all of my relationships have benefited as a result. I am happier and now enjoy far more fulfilling and healthy relationships with friends, family, and romantic partners, given my decisions and the growth I have accomplished in this area.

CHAPTER • 5

Heal the Pain and Shed the Addictions

There is a common characteristic demonstrated by many individuals I have known who experienced prolonged abuse in their lives: Many of us suffer from negative compulsive, habitual behaviors or from full-blown addictions. Many of us turned to pleasure or other distractions as coping mechanisms to deal with the physical and emotional pain that came from abusive experiences. From my experience, it seems the earlier in life an individual started pleasure seeking or using other distractions to deal with the pain associated with abuse, and the longer they remained in an abusive environment, the stronger the hold the compulsive or addictive behaviors will have on the individual.

The particular activity an individual turns to will also dictate the strength of the compulsive or addictive behaviors. Certain recreational drugs come with the price tag of relatively quick dependency and strong addictions in their users —cocaine, heroin, and meth are some examples.

However, addictions can take many forms besides a dependency to a particular substance. Any activity an individual uses, pleasurable or not, to create a temporary release or a distraction from pain can turn into an addiction. Sexual pleasure and the many things related to it (pornography, prostitution, infidelity, aggressive victimization, and masturbation) can all become avenues to addiction. The use of food as a means of distraction can also lead to addictions such as compulsive overeating or eating disorders. The thrill associated with accumulating money and material items can lead to addictive behaviors such as gambling, overspending, or compulsive shopping.

Some addictive behaviors can even appear to be beneficial on the surface, such as someone becoming addicted to their work or career, but this may serve to feed other addictions under the surface, such as the compulsion to make and spend money or to accumulate material wealth and social status. People can become addicted to fame or popularity and may rely on the constant attention and admiration they receive from their social network as a distraction.

Seeking constant sources of adrenaline rushes can also be a form of addiction. Some individuals seem to have a need or compulsion to constantly remain busy, never taking time to relax, unwind, or to be still and quiet. Many of us probably know someone who appears to have an addiction to their smartphone or their social media accounts.

The question arises, then, at what point does engaging in one or any of these behaviors turn from having a life experience to engaging in a compulsive behavior or habit and then to an addiction? Most individuals can take part in many of these experiences without ever being driven by a compulsion or serving as an addiction. I have known many people who experimented with recreational drugs and did not turn into addicts.

Nearly all people enjoy sexual experiences and experiment with masturbation throughout life, which are beneficial and healthy if practiced in moderation. Many people can overeat at times, be described as workaholics, enjoy gambling, occasionally seek adrenaline-producing activities, spend too much money, or accumulate material wealth without being driven by a negative compulsion or an addiction.

I believe addiction is best described along a continuum or on a scale. At one end is an individual who can take part in the various pleasures life has to offer and enjoy them periodically or perhaps even for a prolonged time. The key is they can easily disengage from these behaviors or pleasures without experiencing anxiety or stress; so there is no attachment. And they can pick them up at a later time to be enjoyed again if they so desire.

On the other end of the scale is an individual who is completely consumed by a behavior or habit. They have no self-control and no self-awareness. The pursuit of the substance or habit completely consumes their life and dictates their behaviors on a regular basis and on a grand scale. This pursuit has a drastic effect on the balance in their life: Careers suffer, relationships suffer, responsibilities suffer, spirituality suffers, and their health, wellness, and self-care suffer. The end of this scale is full-blown addiction, and the individual can be described as an addict.

In the middle of these two extremes are compulsive behaviors and habits, which can have varying degrees of intensity. Compulsive behaviors and habits can either be positive or negative, and this is completely dependent on what drives or motivates them.

Based on my experience and from reading spiritual works, I believe if the habit, behavior, or activity is being driven by a negative compulsion or an addiction, then several themes are likely present. Eckhart Tolle, in *The Power of Now*, states plainly:

> Every addiction arises from an unconscious refusal to face and move through your own pain. Every addiction starts with pain and ends with pain. Whatever the substance you are addicted to—alcohol, food, legal or illegal drugs, or a person—you are using something or somebody to cover up your pain. ... Every addiction [brings out the pain and unhappiness that is already in you]. Every addiction reaches a point where it does not work for you anymore, and then you feel the pain more intensely than ever.

A dominating theme of all addictions or negative compulsive behaviors is fear or pain operating in the background. If the behavior or activity is being used as a means to distract from dealing with painful emotions or memories of fearful experiences, then it is not healthy and is not beneficial on the spiritual or emotional level. If fear and avoidance of pain are operating behind the behavior or habit, then I believe it can fairly be described as a negative compulsive behavior or an addiction.

Another indication of addictive energy being present behind an activity is whether the activity is something you truly want to be doing or something you feel you have to be doing. Taking a good hard look at our list of "have to's" from time to time is a good internal check. The important part of this is to be completely truthful in evaluating what the real motivation or intention is behind the "have to's" and determining if these intentions are truly beneficial or not. When a behavior is driven by a negative compulsion—"have to"—and when that compulsion is in the driver's seat, then it may be a sign something behind it is in control other than our higher self.

A good indication of how much control a compulsion has over you lies in the emotional reaction you feel if you try to stop a particular habit or behavior, or if something outside yourself forces the behavior or habit to come to a halt. If an individual cannot stop or change the behavior at will after many attempts, or if a significant amount of anxiety or stress comes to the surface if external circumstances prevent the behavior or habit, these are good signs it may be a negative compulsion or an addiction.

Habits or behaviors driven by a negative compulsion or an addiction have a tendency to throw an individual's life out of balance. When the things we truly want and need in our life—our spirituality, our self-care, our relationships with family, friends, lovers, and children, our hobbies and interests—when these start to suffer and fall away as a result of maintaining obligations toward our "have to's" rather than toward the things we truly care about, this is a sign it is time to take a hard look. Is there really a healthy and balanced desire, motivation, or intention behind the behavior, or is there something negative hidden behind it in control?

In a book of collected writings from Ernest Holmes compiled by Rev. Dr. Jesse Jennings, *The Essential Ernest Holmes*, Holmes discusses the general concept of habits and uses a negative habit—alcoholism—as an example. He states plainly, "Some [habits] express themselves constructively and some destructively." With regard to the destructive habits, Holmes had this to say:

> In most cases the habit, itself, is not the real disease. It is the unconscious attempt to escape from the real disease. The disease itself is some inner emotional state, of which the patient generally is not at all aware, but from which he unconsciously shrinks. He is impelled to seek escape through the act of self-forgetting or self-destruction. If this is the case, it follows that the habit will be healed only when its cause is destroyed. In other words, it is not alcoholism, as though it were a thing in itself, that should be attacked, but the hidden cause back of the addiction that needs to be eradicated.
>
> If the cure is to become a real and lasting healing, it will be accomplished only by first uprooting those hidden and subjective causes which lie back of the actual disease, the elimination of unconscious frustrations, whether they occurred in early youth or later in life. ...

Addiction or negative compulsive behaviors are nothing more than an attempt to cover up or distract ourselves from painful emotions and fearful memories we have suppressed. These painful experiences and memories, and the beliefs associated with them, reside in our subconscious mind. For those of us who have experienced abuse as children or perhaps as young adults through domestic violence from a romantic partner, we likely carry painful emotions and memories that drive us into compulsive and addictive behaviors later in life.

We will never be able to fully overcome any addiction until the fear and pain operating behind it is uprooted and addressed. Attempting to stop the addiction while not attacking the root will cause the addiction to resurface later in life, or a new addiction will take its place. We must expose and confront the fear and pain operating at the subconscious level to truly heal the addiction. Once the fear and pain have been confronted, processed, and released, the addictive and compulsive behaviors no longer serve a purpose, and they are much easier to deal with. They may even fall away completely on their own once the pain is healed.

My Struggles with Addiction

I never fell completely off the cliff into a full-blown addiction, but I came very close. There were several interwoven addictive or compulsive behaviors I operated with throughout my life, which I now realize persisted for about twenty-five years. I was aware of the addictive behaviors for a long time but failed repeatedly in my attempts to stop them. At times, I was aware of these compulsions. At other times, I was not aware the compulsions were driving me until after I had gone through and come out the other side of a painful experience that resulted. I was aware for many years that I used these compulsive behaviors to deal in some way with the pain from child abuse. But the actual, specific fear or pain operating under the surface did not come to my awareness until my mid-thirties. This is when I was finally able to overcome these habits operating so strongly. I had to identify the specific fear and the emotions associated with that fear, and I had to identify where it all came from, before I was able to put myself in a place where I could consciously heal it and shed the behaviors.

For twenty-five years, I sought the attention and affection of women as a means to distract myself from the fear and pain of the abusive experiences I had as a child. I also turned to sexual pleasure as a distraction, and my pursuit of these two coping mechanisms were often intertwined with each other. I recall, even as young as ten years old, I constantly wanted a girlfriend. There was a particular girl in my class at my elementary school who I obsessed over for nearly four years.

This girl had no romantic interest in or attraction to me whatsoever, yet I continued to pursue her and obsess over her in my mind despite rejection after rejection. Once in high school, my fantasies shifted to other girls. However, I had absolutely no self-confidence and low self-esteem, which plummeted to its all-time low in high school. My ability to get a girlfriend at that time was nonexistent. I was particularly terrified of the girls I found to be physically attractive and who were popular. I had so little confidence in myself, I could barely muster enough courage to even say hello. I did not have my first girlfriend until I was sixteen years old, and she only remained with me for a few months.

After I graduated high school, I started to become aware of—and quite surprised by—the fact that there were actually many girls who found me attractive and saw me as a good person, which boosted my confidence. Once I started getting girlfriends, I almost always had one or was in pursuit of one. This continued until my mid-thirties but took on the characteristic of jumping into romantic relationships almost immediately following divorces.

The use of sexual pleasure as a distraction also came at an early age. I was exposed to pornography when I was ten years old, and I started masturbating at that time. My older brother had a friend whose parents had an extensive collection of pornography and sex toys. One day, several of us young boys went to his house while his parents were not home and indulged in pornographic videos for several hours. We were way too young to be exposed to pornography, and I began masturbating the same day I was exposed to these films.

I masturbated obsessively and excessively when I was a teen. I did it most frequently when there were stressful situations in my home—either when my parents were fighting or following abusive experiences. I became obsessed with sex, but due to my inability to approach girls or get girlfriends when I was a teen, I masturbated to escape. I loathed those male friends around me who were able to maintain steady girlfriends and have regular sex.

The habitual masturbation had a toxic side effect, causing guilt and shame due to influences from the Catholic church. I was taught as a junior in my Catholic high school that masturbation was a mortal sin, and if we died with a mortal sin on our soul without confession, we would go to hell. I completely believed this, yet I was terrified and embarrassed to speak to a priest about my habit. When I finally had the courage to do so in a formal confession, I realized I still could not seem to stop the behavior. At the time, it felt like an addiction. I would try after a confession and make it two to three weeks, then the urges would overpower me, and I would eventually start masturbating again.

At times, I would go on a binge, as some people do with drugs or alcohol, and repeat the act multiple times a day over a several-day period. I would then be wracked with guilt and shame. This was a repetitive pattern I lived over and over through most of my teen years. Little did I know at the time, masturbation is a completely normal and healthy aspect of one's sexuality, and most people masturbate on a regular basis at various times in their lives. I had no awareness of this at the time, and I thought I was the only person in the world who engaged in this so-called disgusting and sinful behavior.

I began developing unhealthy, superstitious beliefs around the masturbation and around God. I believed, if I could not stop the behavior, God would somehow punish me. I believed the way in which I was being punished was that the attention or admiration of women, which I was always desperately seeking, would be withheld from me. When I decided to pursue a girl, I recall I would stop masturbating completely in hopes of improving my chances. If I had a girlfriend, I also did not engage in the behavior out of fear that the relationship would fall apart. It seemed if I was getting physical attention and affection from a girl, I was quite happy. But if I was rejected or the girl broke up with me, I would sink into a depressed state and go on a binge of self-pleasuring again. Even as an adult, because of the many years during which I associated guilt and shame with masturbation, it took me a long time to finally develop a healthy relationship with my own sexuality, to accept my sex drive, and to be able to enjoy masturbation without negative emotions surfacing.

Addiction's Influence in My Romantic Relationships

My addictive patterns continued into adulthood when romantic relationships started becoming more involved, more serious, and more sexual. Physical and sexual intimacy simply replaced the masturbation. I was always either in pursuit of or involved in relationships with girlfriends throughout my freshman year of college. I met my first wife, Rebecca, sophomore year and remained in a relationship with her for thirteen years. As I mentioned previously, I was involved in an affair with a woman while Rebecca and I were going through our divorce, and then Anna came into the picture just two weeks after the affair ended.

There was a constant pattern of jumping into one relationship after another and giving myself little time to process or heal. Friends who engaged in similar behaviors jokingly described me and themselves as "serial monogamists." Covering up fear and pain was certainly not the sole reason for me getting into these relationships or for seeking physical pleasure from women—after all, I was a typical male in my late teens and early twenties. But I now realize the fear and pain always had been operating under the surface, which led to destructive behaviors and repetitive themes in my relationships.

During our marriage, Rebecca's episodes of depression and anxiety occurred off and on, and they often lasted a year or more. Another source of conflict and resentment was my higher sex drive. Her episodes of depression and anxiety meant she was emotionally unavailable to me, and during these episodes she could not be truly present. Additionally, her sex drive plummeted even more, and the physical aspect of our relationship declined significantly. In essence, I lost both of my coping mechanisms—the attention and affection I desired from a woman was gone, and the physical aspect of sexual pleasure was practically gone. During these times, I turned back to the obsessive and excessive masturbation as a coping mechanism, and I kept this behavior hidden from Rebecca. I had a tendency of doing it multiple times a day, and sometimes every day—whether I needed to or not. There were times I did not even want to masturbate or felt no sexual urge or desire to do so, but I did it anyway as something to do to distract myself from whatever circumstances were occurring or from whatever painful emotions I was experiencing.

Rebecca began falling into her first depression, I believe, shortly after we were married during my last year of graduate school. When we moved across the country to the Pacific Northwest for my first job out of graduate school, she fell into a deep depression. My work required me to travel quite frequently, and I began engaging in a new but related behavior that became quite compulsive over the years: I began pursuing other women when I worked out of town.

I would often go to restaurants and bars to flirt with female staff or customers. Early on, I did not put much effort into it. I would start a conversation to see where it would go and to gauge a woman's interest. But I always carried the intention or hope that the situation could evolve into a sexual encounter. If it did not go anywhere or I did not see any interest from the woman, I quickly gave up. However, toward the last two or three years of our marriage, the compulsive urges intensified as my resentment over the circumstances in our marriage intensified, and I began pursuing women far more regularly and with much stronger intentions. If I was working out of town, I was constantly seeking one-night stands and trying to pick up women in bars. If I found a woman who was interested in talking with me or getting to know me, I would try to continue flirting with her or pursuing her over a period of several days. I was not being honest with these women about my true circumstances, that I was married and had a child at home. I also stopped wearing my wedding ring any time I traveled for work.

My behavior during this time became very obsessive. I was out of control and did not care much or give much regard to consequences that could arise—the potential for a wrecked marriage, home, and family; broken hearts, dishonesty, and deceit to the women I was chasing; or the possibility of picking up a sexually transmitted disease. None of it mattered to me at the time. I was essentially in self-destruct mode, as Ernest Holmes describes above. There were times I even considered hiring escorts when I was on the road, but thankfully I did not ever take that plunge.

Every time my attempts failed to produce a sexual encounter, I was back in my hotel room masturbating obsessively, often supplemented with pornography. The honest truth is, I felt like a complete loser and a failure when I did this. I knew I had a problem, and I even sought help from a therapist for a time. Either this therapist did not realize or take seriously the addictive behaviors I was engaging in, or perhaps I was not fully honest or open because I was not ready to change or face what was operating underneath. Either way, I continued these behaviors shortly after attending the therapy sessions.

I thank God now I did not accomplish my desires during those times. I truly believe if I had been successful and managed to have sexual encounters during these pursuits, I would have fallen off the cliff into the world of full-blown sex addiction.

I brought these behaviors to Rebecca's attention when we were seeking marriage counseling for the third or fourth time. This was the final year of our marriage, and I wanted to come clean and work on the marriage. But by this time, too much damage had been done, and she was experiencing resentment of her own. She did not seem willing to put forth any effort, and given what I was doing during the times when she was at her lowest points, I fully understand her decision. When she was honest with me and told me she did not want to try to work on the relationship from her end, I decided to leave her.

I made the decision to divorce Rebecca six months before I finally announced my intention to her. She was finishing graduate school, and I wanted her to graduate before I notified her of my decision. During three of those last six months, I met another woman who almost immediately started flirting with me, and I immediately picked up on her energy and started pursuing her. As part of her culture, she was in an arranged marriage, in which she was quite unhappy. I learned from her that she experienced physical abuse from her spouse on a number of occasions. She told me at the time she was also considering a divorce, so I rationalized it was not really an affair. We quickly became romantically involved and were fully engaged in secret meetings, phone calls, texts, emails, etc., behind our respective spouses' and families' backs. After our first sexual encounter; however, she experienced a tremendous amount of guilt, and it became clear to me that she had not fully made up her mind to leave her spouse. I tried to convince her on many occasions to move forward with the divorce, but she would not.

We eventually both agreed to stop the affair and cease contact with one another. Initially, this was difficult for me to do. I had a strong temptation to continue seeing her, strictly for the physical component, even though I knew with certainty she was not leaving her husband and would not be truly available to me. I was even aware of the risk to her if he found out, given his tendency to physically abuse her, but I dismissed this. Again, I was in self-destruct mode, and I was willing to screw up the lives of others in my pursuits.

A couple of weeks after this affair ended, Anna came back into my life by sending that serendipitous email to me after nine years of no contact, and I avidly pursued her. I had barely started the divorce process with Rebecca at this time. In a matter of only four months, Anna and I found ourselves expecting a child before the divorce process was even completed. We were married only two months after the decree came from the courts.

What is clear to me now is that I was fairly obsessed with being involved with a woman and, in the process, created a lot of drama for myself. Several of my coworkers at the time threw me a baby shower for the arrival of my second child, and they jokingly referred to it as the "Chris's-life-is-complicated" party.

In addition to ignoring unhealthy dynamics in the early days of Anna's and my relationship, I also ignored obvious signs from my own body in my pursuit of her. I was under so much stress from all I had going on, I could not function sexually. So, I asked my doctor to prescribe me Viagra, which did the trick just fine and allowed me to continue pursuing my habits. It was more comfortable for me to be involved with someone, especially with regular sex occurring, than it was for me to be alone, apparently even if the relationship was unhealthy and toxic.

I recognized the discomfort associated with the thought of being alone if I had to end the marriage with Anna, and I had a lot of anxiety about not having a sexual partner. Despite the high level of conflict that characterized our relationship, for the most part we both had fairly high sex drives and could still enjoy the physical aspect of the relationship with one another quite frequently. I also doubted my ability to be a single parent to two boys, especially one as young as my second son. I had to reach a point at which my safety and well-being were at high risk before I got out. In other words, I essentially had to be forced to end the relationship. The fear of potential consequences for remaining involved with this woman had to outweigh my fear of loneliness.

Within a short time of ending that relationship, my self-awareness developed enough to see clearly that I had remained in an unsafe environment and toxic relationship, in part for the sex and in part because of a discomfort associated with being alone. I started to question whether or not I had a sex addiction.

Within a couple of months of our separation, I had to go out of town for work twice. On both trips, the urges returned to seek out a woman, similar to what I did during my first marriage. These urges had been completely absent during my relationship with Anna because the sex was frequent. But as soon it was not available, the urges returned. This alarmed me. Having seen the risk I just put myself in, I made the decision to stop this behavior. I spent several months praying, meditating, and journaling around this issue. It was not until I felt comfortable that I was not being driven by sexual urges that I started dating again. However, I do not believe I gave it enough time.

Uprooting My Pain

It became clear to me later, I still had not actually become aware of and uprooted the specific pain operating under the surface. The need for additional healing became apparent after I made a decision to end a twelve-month relationship with a woman who I was fond of, who was extremely kind and good to me, but who unfortunately did not have the time or availability I wanted for a committed romantic relationship.

Several things happened within me shortly after making the decision to end that relationship. At first, I felt empowered and proud of myself for being able to communicate my needs and boundaries. I was happy I had the ability to walk away from a relationship in which I knew my needs and preferences could not be met. A previous version of me would have hung in there, clinging, trying to control, change, or fix the circumstances. I would have remained in the relationship as long as possible and built up resentment as a result of my own failure to communicate and honor my needs, preferences, and boundaries. This previous version of me would also have remained in a relationship characterized by dissatisfying circumstances just for the sex. By leaving this relationship, I felt the growth and progress in my decision to honor and take care of myself.

However, the second thing that occurred within me, I was not expecting at all. I became completely overwhelmed by panic and anxiety within a couple of days after the relationship ended. Once the realization hit that the relationship was over and I was once again without a woman to spend time with, I had an immediate urge to attempt to quickly patch things up and continue as things were. I also experienced a simultaneous and compulsive urge to immediately venture out and start trying to find someone else. This greatly concerned me, because I believed I had moved beyond all of this. It seems now I may have fooled myself into believing this, or perhaps residual triggers arose because I had not actually uprooted the real pain operating under the surface. Regardless of what it was, I knew I still had work to do, and I did not allow either of these urges to push me into a poor decision.

For the first time in my life, I decided to just sit with these emotions—the panic and anxiety that arose within me—and I allowed myself to feel them. I meditated while feeling them, in an attempt to discover where they came from and what caused them. Also for the first time, I truly understood what I had learned from classes at my church and from reading spiritual work from several authors—what it means to just be with my emotions and allow them to come out and flow through me and be released.

In doing this, I finally unearthed and uprooted the fear and pain operating in my subconscious, driving these compulsive behaviors and urges to seek out women, sex, and romantic relationships.

Through several meditation sessions, it became clear to me I had done all of this since I was a child. As a result of the abuse I experienced as a child, I had a persistent feeling of loneliness and isolation throughout my childhood and teen years. Those feelings and the pain associated with them were more crippling, more debilitating, and more excruciating than *any* of the pain I had ever experienced from the actual physical beatings I took from my father or from the physical abuse I experienced from my mother. That loneliness and isolation nearly drove me to suicide in my late teens. The fear of those emotions, the avoidance of having them resurface, the pain I suppressed into my subconscious—this is what was driving these compulsive behaviors that had operated so strongly in most of my adult life. This is why I sought women, relationships, and sex so obsessively.

In my meditations, I finally faced and confronted my fear and painful emotions. I allowed myself to feel every part of it. Every experience and memory from my childhood and teen years when I felt those emotions flooded into my mind all at once it seemed. The pain was excruciating, but in allowing myself to feel the pain, I experienced a profound healing. There was a warmth, a presence, and a peace within me that immediately rose up and overpowered all of it, took it all away, released it, and completely removed that burden from me.

Once I confronted and healed my pain, the compulsive behaviors no longer had as strong a hold on me. With the self-awareness I developed through processing those emotions and identifying where it all came from, I found it much easier from that day forward to be the "silent watcher" and to listen to, watch, and feel the compulsions still trying to operate in my egoic mind.

I also experienced a physical healing in my body, I believe, as a side effect of this pain being removed. I had been diagnosed with high blood pressure during the high-conflict phase of my relationship with Anna, and I was put on prescription medication. I never believed this condition belonged to me, and I never owned it. I knew from the beginning, I could heal it. Over the months prior to my realization, I began weaning myself off of the medication, only to be frustrated by seeing high readings when I would have my blood pressure checked. After my healing experience, my blood pressure levels began falling, and I weaned off of the medication completely and have never had to go back on it.

The other pattern that became quite clear to me was the type of women I chose to pursue or who I drew into my life. Science of Mind principles teach that the beliefs or emotions operating within us, particularly at the subconscious level, send a signal out, and there is a response to bring us circumstances and experiences that allow us to continue thinking/feeling the same things—until we decide to change it. *Every* woman I have ever pursued in my life or engaged in relationships with was not available to me in some form or another. And this now makes perfect sense to me. I constantly pursued with a fear of loneliness and isolation operating in my subconscious, so it is logical to see how I would draw in individuals or engage in relationships with women who would allow me to continue experiencing loneliness and isolation.

Ernest Hemmingway wrote, "I have been alone while I was with many girls and that is the way you can be most lonely."

This was apparently my life's mantra until recently, but I was not aware of it operating. Every one of the girlfriends I had before my first wife were still in love with ex-boyfriends they had recently broken up with, and I was a rebound who was eventually dropped when they could reengage with those individuals. Rebecca, in dealing with her own baggage, struggled with depression through most of our marriage, and I felt more lonely than ever during those times with her and while I was out woman-chasing during my work travel. I knew the woman with whom I engaged in an affair was not fully available to me, yet I pursued her anyway. Anna suffered from her own core beliefs of being unlovable and having a fear of abandonment. She pushed away people who showed her love and affection. The last woman I engaged in a relationship with before the realization finally hit me was clearly too busy with her own demands in life to give me the attention I wanted.

The Effects of My Healing

I have spoken with several recovering addicts about their experiences with addiction and recovery. The best advice I received is that though you heal it and move beyond it, you must have a constant sense of self-awareness around it. The cravings subside but never go away completely. The temptations and urges have a tendency to linger and rise up at other times, especially during stressful circumstances.

I have noticed this in myself, but it eventually became far easier to control rather than allowing it to control me. I also learned that we have to be gentle with ourselves and maintain a sense of compassion if we temporarily backslide, and this compassion makes it easier to re-center and continue in the direction of our goals.

A great piece of advice given to me by a recovering alcoholic was that she made a list of ten things she will do before she decides to take a drink. So I made two lists for myself. One was a list of things I would do instead of going out and chasing women if I felt those urges, and two was a list of things I wanted to know about a woman and experience with her before I engaged in sexual intimacy.

Science of Mind teaches that when you change your energy and your subconscious mind and start sending out a new signal, new and different circumstances appear. I am grateful to share that I have operated in a much healthier manner in regards to dating and romantic relationships since I have done this inner work. As a result of these shifts in my energy and behavior, I attracted a healthy, compatible, kind and loving woman, with whom I enjoy a romantic partnership. This has been the most fulfilling change that emerged from engaging in this healing work.

I now also can say with honesty, I have a healthy relationship with my own sexuality. If I need to masturbate, I do it, I have fun with it, and there is no guilt or shame. It is well-balanced now and does not interfere with or take away from any other areas of my life. I also find no need to do so now that I am involved in a healthy romantic relationship.

Before I found this woman, I developed the ability to walk away from other relationships when my boundaries were not respected or my needs were not being met. I refused to try to force relationships with women who I found were not a good fit. In the past, if I found a woman attractive and she was interested in me, that was all that existed on my checklist, and I would dive in headfirst and throw all caution to the wind. I continually found myself over-compromising my boundaries and engaging in self-sacrifice in my relationships. My checklist now is much more thorough, and I have done well in both communicating and maintaining my boundaries. I know with certainty that I have healed and moved beyond my pain and shed these negative compulsions.

Author's Note for Treating Addiction

Please understand that addressing or treating an actual addiction is beyond the scope of this book. Drug or alcohol abuse, sex addiction, or any other addiction can be treated and overcome. There are abundant resources available to individuals who wish to seek help. I have known many who have succeeded in overcoming addictions through twelve-step programs and by joining support groups with other recovering addicts.

If you are struggling with an addiction and wish to defeat it, you must do the work necessary to expose and uproot the pain. Then, to treat the addiction, seek help from loving family or friends, therapists, counselors, church groups, or doctors. Know and believe: Help is out there, then start asking for it and looking for it. The avenue that will work best for you will manifest itself if you set the intention and do your part.

I know with certainty that anyone who wishes to heal and who holds the intention to heal has the ability and the power within themselves to do so. I also know Spirit provides all the resources and support, once an intention is firmly set in the mind and heart.

Confront and heal your pain and fears, and shed your addictions.

CHAPTER • 6

Develop Self-Awareness

The preceding chapters each invite readers to look at and develop a sense of awareness around several personal aspects: to tune into pent-up memories and painful emotions you may harbor, to realize the persistence of resentment or anger toward abusers in your life, to identify where boundaries are required and to see the need to establish them in your relationships, and to identify fear/pain operating under the surface and the resulting addictive behaviors you may experience. Those who have experienced abuse need to develop a sense of self-awareness around all of these traits if they want to heal.

In the second part of this book, I describe how I used a variety of spiritual practices to assist in developing my own self-awareness around these issues. I also describe how I used these practices to heal. The awareness is only the first step, but it is a completely necessary step. We cannot heal or change anything about ourselves if we have no awareness of it. So if we truly desire healing and change in our lives, then we must develop self-awareness.

Self-awareness really needs to be defined in two different ways. Ernest Holmes in his book, *The Science of Mind*, discusses the "Self": the true essence of an individual, their soul, their spirit, the incorruptible and immortal part of us that is connected with and possesses all the qualities of God. And he describes the "self," which in essence is our ego, the uncontrolled prattling of our minds, our personalities, our unconscious habits and behaviors. Developing awareness of both of these aspects, Self and self, comes through the use of two necessary spiritual practices: being present and meditating.

Two influential books for me in understanding these concepts to develop my own self-awareness were *The Power of Now* by Eckhart Tolle and *Breaking the Habit of Being Yourself* by Dr. Joe Dispenza. One of the primary topics discussed in *The Power of Now* is being present, existing in the now, rather than worrying about the future or experiencing regret, shame, or guilt over the past.

By being present in the now, we tap into or bring out our true self. One of the most important principles Tolle discusses in his book is that we are not our thoughts; we are not our bodies; we are not our personalities; we are not our emotions. Rather, our true essence, what we truly are, is what Tolle calls the Silent Watcher, the Observer, the One who has the ability to watch or listen to the thoughts, the One who feels the emotions. When we are present, we consciously choose to watch our thoughts and feel our emotions in the moment, and then we become tuned in to a higher power within us, the "Self" as Holmes discusses in *The Science of Mind*.

This technique requires continual and repetitive practice and awareness. In essence, what is involved is stopping what you are doing or are about to do, stopping what you are saying or are about to say, and watching and listening to your own thoughts, feeling your emotions as they occur, or feeling your entire body or any part of it in the moment. An amazing thing happens when you make a conscious choice to stop and look at, listen to, or watch your thoughts. The same thing happens when you consciously tune into and focus on feeling your entire body, any part of your body, or feel an emotional state as it occurs within your body. Within a short time of initiating any of these practices, you stop thinking. The longer you can maintain the concentration to consciously *feel,* the longer you can go without thinking, and the more present you become. In those moments of not thinking, not analyzing, not judging, not planning or worrying about something in the future, when no thought is occurring at all—this is when you are truly present. Rather than thinking, you are experiencing, soaking in, and feeling everything occurring all around you and within you. When you are truly present, you can *feel* something within you. What you are feeling is your true self and your true essence.

One of the main purposes of this technique is to increase your awareness to this essence within. It is not something that comes forth in thoughts. It is not a tangible idea or words formulated in your mind. It is not something you can physically touch, see, or hear. Rather, it is something you can *feel.* In those moments when you consciously choose to watch your thoughts and emotions, when you have practiced the technique often enough to cease the constant stream of thought, you start to feel something within and all around you. It is a power, a presence, and an energy that is always there, has always been there, and will always be there. It is unmistakable, undeniable, and is what you truly are.

It comes at first in brief glimpses, because it can be difficult to train our minds to shut down and remain shut down for long stretches of time. But the more you access and tune into this power by being present, the more you turn off your thoughts by watching them, the more familiar this power becomes to you and the more often you can feel it. It begins to grow and expand. The feeling of it grows stronger and more certain with each moment you access it. Your awareness to it increases the more often you tune into it.

Continual practice of this technique also causes the duration of those brief moments to expand into more prolonged experiences of joy, bliss, and deep peace. This is precisely what is meant in the New Testament when Luke wrote, "Behold, the Kingdom of God is within you" (Luke 17:21 The New King James Version).

Identifying and Becoming Aware of Our Ego

Practicing this technique also is a useful and, I believe, necessary tool to expose our ego and become aware of its patterns and erroneous beliefs. The more we watch and become aware of the ego, the less and less of a hold the ego can maintain over us. As we watch our thoughts and consciously feel our emotions in the moment more frequently, our automatic reactions and behavioral tendencies derived from our ego and from our limiting core beliefs start to become less and less automatic. Ultimately those reactions and behavioral patterns we find undesirable in ourselves start to fall away the more we bring our awareness to them as they occur in our day-to-day experiences. Watching our thoughts and emotional reactions as they occur within us, being aware of them in the moment, provides us with opportunities to make conscious choices of how we wish to respond in the moment, rather than being on autopilot and reacting automatically and unconsciously to external stimuli.

Dr. Joe Dispenza's book, *Breaking the Habit of Being Yourself,* provides practices and techniques to expose what Dispenza refers to as our "ego self" and bring it front and center to look at. The book provides tools to reduce the ego's level of control in our lives. He also delves into the neuroscience and biochemistry occurring within our bodies that can hinder our attempts to change. Dispenza explains that the ego self is responsible for the habitual behaviors, emotional reactions, and thought and belief patterns we operate with to bring experiences into our lives. He provides tools to change the undesirable aspects we carry within us that attract undesirable circumstances. He further explains how changing these aspects of ourselves brings about changes in the experiences we draw into our lives, which is in line with the principles of Science of Mind.

For those of us who have gone through abuse, one of our goals in developing self-awareness is to identify and bring to the surface the limiting core beliefs we adopted from the experiences. We also need to identify any undesirable behaviors or habits we operate with on a regular basis related to our limiting core beliefs. Once the core beliefs are exposed, we can uproot them and change them. From there, changing the undesirable characteristics becomes more manageable. Without exposing and uprooting the core beliefs, however, change and healing, in my experience, are not possible.

My Journey of Self-Awareness

My own journey toward awareness of my true self and my ego self began many years ago during the end of my marriage with Rebecca. I was making attempts to discover and eradicate bad habits I showed up with in our relationship, but I did not know at that time where they came from.

The journey really took off when I was exposed to Science of Mind and began taking classes through Centers for Spiritual Living. The first class I took, "Beyond Limits," coincided with when I first began a meditation practice. I consider this the beginning of my personal awakening, the initiation of developing my full awareness to my ego and my true essence. Meditation allowed me to experience and feel my true essence and to get in touch with it. It created separation from my ego, which allowed me to observe as an outsider would.

Through time, my own intuition revealed to me in meditation that I adopted and carried around a limiting core belief that I was no good or not a good person. I know with certainty that belief was adopted partially, if not entirely, through my experiences of child abuse, bullying, and neglect.

My awareness of all the ways I showed up in life related to that belief filtered in over several years by using a regular meditation practice and other spiritual practices. I chose to increase my awareness so I could understand nearly all aspects of my behaviors and why I showed up the way I did. My destructive habits, my beneficial habits, my automatic emotional reactions and behavioral patterns—I dug up where all of it originated. I was actually shocked to discover I had been doing all these things and maintaining all of these persistent patterns since I was a small child.

This limiting belief of being no good that I carried with me for so long manifested itself in nearly every aspect of my life. For example, I was critical and judgmental of others, primarily those closest to me. The critical and judgmental behavior was essentially a way for me to prop myself up, because at the core, I did not like myself. This was a major contributor to the demise of my marriage to Rebecca. I also often showed up with a bit of arrogance and an inflated ego in my work and career related to this. Over time, this started to have a negative impact on my working relationships, and I realized a change was necessary.

I became a perfectionist early in childhood and consistently earned straight As throughout elementary school, high school, college and in graduate school. Being academically successful was actually a way I could prove to myself or to others that I was a good person. While I deem this a beneficial habit that came as a means of dealing with this core belief; the pressure I placed on myself for perfectionism did not serve me.

I caused myself a considerable amount of stress in college to perform at a high level, and I believe my life was out of balance. I did not give myself much time for fun, self-care, or socializing. I was similarly out of balance in my career, working almost all of the time until I nearly burned out and changed jobs.

I also placed this burden onto others in my life, as I alluded to above, by using criticism and judgmental behavior. I was blessed by my hard work and achieved success in my career, so this characteristic carried a benefit with it. However, I had to learn how to balance it, keep my ego out of the way of my hard work, give myself time for fun and self-care, and erase the judgmental and critical thoughts that came from comparing myself to others.

This belief of being no good was extremely prominent in my social life throughout elementary school, in high school, and in my college years. I had low self-esteem and was extremely awkward socially. I did not believe I was any good. I did not like myself, so how could anyone else possibly like me? I had few friends and often felt lonely and isolated. I found it extremely difficult to function in social settings with more than a couple of people without feeling overwhelmed and awkward. I had no skills or desire to approach anyone new in conversation or in attempts to get to know them, because I believed from the get-go that they would not like me. I carried this tendency with me even as a young child. I always preferred to play alone rather than try to meet new friends. In elementary school, I was picked on by older children because of my awkwardness. I responded in kind by picking on and bullying others. In high school, I was a loner, often picked on, with few friends and practically no social life.

In college, I adopted the skills to "fake it until you make it." I learned to show up inauthentically or in ways I believed people wanted me to be so I could be accepted or feel like I had friends. Alcohol always helped this, it seemed, and I turned to partying and drinking to allow me to loosen up. With alcohol, I found it easy to be a fun and entertaining person, or to engage in the group mentality so I would feel accepted and maintain friendships. Most of these friendships were shallow and not characterized by true authenticity or intimacy, and few of them lasted. The only ongoing friendships were with individuals I truly opened up to and shared with on deeper and more intimate levels.

Developing my awareness also brought to the surface the realization of the resentment I carried with me all my life and the effects it had on me. The core belief I had adopted was also a contributing force that drove me to seek the attention, admiration, and affection of women that I have previously discussed. I essentially sought to build up my self-worth through the attention of women.

This limiting core belief resulted in another tendency I carried that I have alluded to throughout the preceding chapters: my tendency toward defensiveness and taking things said to me personally and as criticism. Since I was a young child, I took any correction directed at me as deep and personal criticism. I would defend myself vehemently. I recall our report cards when I was in elementary school. The left side of the report card contained the school subjects with our grades; the right side contained information related to our behavior. Check marks on the right side of our report card were an indication of areas in which our behavior was not acceptable or needed work. I consistently had a check mark in a box labeled "Does Not Accept Correction Well." I fought with every teacher and with my parents over any correction addressed to me. The way I fought was with defensiveness or trying to prove that their accusation against me was wrong or misinformed, and that I was right. My parents shut me down by getting more aggressive and abusing me. My teachers did not resort to this option, thankfully, but they certainly found me a difficult child to work with.

This characteristic stuck with me into adulthood, and it is still something I need to devote a significant amount of attention toward to avoid engaging in old habits. When I was a young adult, my reactions would often be characterized by shouting, using profanity, and completely losing my self-control and temper. As I developed more awareness around it, I had far better control over my reactions. But this trait resurfaced and became especially prominent in my marriage to Anna, and I also realized its role with my relationship to my mother. I soon became aware that this characteristic was the primary reason I remained engaged in conflict with people who I had close relationships with.

Essentially, if someone would criticize me or just try to bring up a concern, and I chose to perceive it as criticism, I would literally dig into every detail about the circumstances. I used my memories and, if they existed, dug up old emails, cited specific details in previous conversations, dug out journal entries or letters to prove these individuals wrong, to show them that their accusatory or critical statements were exaggerated, misinformed, or just plain lies. I was good at this because I was gifted with a near-photographic memory and could recall any detail I needed to support my stance to make me right and to make them wrong. I realize now how misguided this is, and how invalidating it is for the other person in the relationship.

Although I may have believed my stance to be true, and although I may have believed my side or my perception was the truth, none of this served me at all. It took me a long time and a lot of conflict to learn the lesson: People form their own perceptions of you or of events around you, and they are going to believe what they want to believe. They are going to see things the way they want to see them, in the way that best supports their perceptions, whether they are right, correct, and factual—or not. Don Miguel Ruiz states it truthfully in his book, *The Four Agreements,* and he devotes an entire chapter to this concept: "Don't Take Anything Personally."

I now believe there is really no need to defend against any attack or accusation unless there is a potential to truly cause personal loss or physical harm. In my experience, these kinds of situations are few and far between, and they can be easily distinguished from the types brought on by conflict-addicted bullies by using one's self-awareness.

I have learned that an even softer approach is to truly attempt to maintain an awareness that if someone is bringing up a concern to me, or even showing up in a critical manner because they are clumsy in their delivery, there are real feelings behind their words. This person is feeling something, probably unpleasant, and my actions or behaviors may have something to do with it. Rather than taking it personally, I now feel it is my role to truly try to understand and validate the other person's feelings behind their words. It is less important for me to be right or to win. Our relationships become far more rewarding when we truly seek to remain curious and try to understand what someone else is feeling or experiencing, even when they are bringing up some issue that is related to our own behaviors.

One of the real wake-up calls related to my own self-awareness that jarred me was a day when I caught myself repeating some of the same behaviors and tactics toward my son, Dillon, that my parents had used on me—namely, suppressing his emotions. I vividly remember catching myself experiencing anger over him crying or being upset at something and essentially telling him to stop it, that there was nothing to be upset or to cry over. Soon after this incident, many events from my own past when my parents had done this to me flooded into my mind. This is, unfortunately, a common characteristic of abuse. It is generational and transfers from one generation to the next until someone stops, chooses to wake up, and makes conscious changes in how they show up and how they move forward in raising their own children. I am so grateful I began developing my awareness when he was a young child, so I could stop these patterns from projecting onto him and onto my younger son, Michael, before the patterns became engrained in me as habit.

Doing the work I did to develop my self-awareness was not easy, and it did not happen overnight. It took me several years to dig into myself and bring my awareness to these traits, habits, behaviors, and reactions that did not serve me spiritually or emotionally. These habits and behaviors had a negative impact on my relationships, and they drained me as a human being. I realized the belief I was no good or not a good person no longer served me. I uprooted it; I changed it; I shed it; and I continually work to change the habits associated with it. I healed, and I am so much better off for doing this work. I am truly happy and feel free. I am highly successful and sought after in my workplace. I am surrounded by healthy and supportive individuals with whom I maintain close relationships. My boys are loved, cared for, and well off emotionally, physically, and spiritually with me as their father and guide.

I can say with absolute honesty, I now have the life I want.

The Benefits of Going Within

I will close this chapter and Part 1 of this book with these words: Developing self-awareness requires us to go within, and going within is both one of the most challenging and one of the most rewarding tasks we can undertake. This activity, this technique is the heart and soul of the Science of Mind spiritual philosophy.

If we truly desire to heal or change something in our lives, we must go within. If we desire to bring forth a purposeful vision or goal for any area of our life—career, relationships, service, health and wellness, spirituality—we must go within. If we truly wish to live by an ethical code of values, to show up in life with authenticity and integrity, then we must go within.

Going within and developing our self-awareness is one of the most challenging tasks we can undertake because it requires us to be completely honest and direct with ourselves. It requires a level of honesty and integrity with ourselves that we may not be ready for. It is difficult to look at habitual behaviors we or others around us do not like, or that we do not wish to keep. It is difficult to be honest with ourselves about these habits, how they truly affect us, how they affect others around us; and it is difficult to identify where they came from. It is also painful and uncomfortable to go within and dig up old memories, hurtful experiences that may have left scars, and limiting beliefs about ourselves. It is not easy to see and be honest about how these beliefs and related experiences may be playing out in our lives.

Just as physical healing of an injury is painful, so is emotional healing. From my experience, I believe the emotional healing is far more painful. But the pain is necessary, and once released, there is room for light, love, blessings, and gifts. These flow into our lives much on their own when we do this work.

Going within and developing self-awareness allows us to see the critic, the judge, the voice who wants to speak up and criticize, condemn, or bring shame, guilt, and regret as we try to heal or be honest with ourselves. As we go within to pursue a vision or a goal, we can hear the same voice telling us we can't, won't, shouldn't, and are not good enough.

Going within and developing self-awareness is one of the most rewarding things we can do. This task, this technique we use to watch our thoughts, to look at our habits, behaviors, and reactions; to dig up deeply held core beliefs buried in our subconscious and see where they came from and how they are playing out in our lives—this very technique connects us with and tunes us into our higher self, the presence and power within us, our true essence, our spirit and soul. The One who is doing the watching, the observing, the digging without judgment or criticism—this is who and what we truly are. The more we go within and do this type of work, the more we connect with and become familiar with the higher power within us, the more it operates in our lives front and center.

That power heals everything and anything. When we go within as the silent watcher and unearth those old hurts, deep scars, painful emotions and memories, we need not fear. Initially there is pain, but because we are connected with the higher power within us while we do this work, our pain is quickly released and replaced with love, warmth, kindness, and an overwhelming and overpowering sense of peace and serenity. The healing occurs, and we are left whole and repaired.

When the voice and the critic arise when we go within, we should give thanks. Because as we go within as the silent watcher, as our higher selves, we shine a bright light directly on that voice, on the critic, on our ego, exposing it to us so we can watch it, see it, listen to it, and know it for what it is. When it comes back, as it always does, it becomes more and more familiar and easier to dismantle each time.

When the changes start occurring, when there is measured progress, when habits truly fall away, when you can *feel* the healing and the release of emotional baggage, when you begin conscious steps toward your visions and goals—then you become empowered. You have accessed and tuned into a power within you that you realize can do anything, can heal anything, and can accomplish anything. When you access and live with this power front and center, you truly start living, thriving, and accomplishing. The blessings, the relationships, the spiritual gifts, and the abundance flow in easily, like water.

I encourage you to do this work. Go within, develop your self-awareness and your Self-awareness, and begin enjoying the benefits and blessings awaiting you.

This work requires a commitment to consistent and regular spiritual practice. It requires daily effort and work, and it cannot be stopped or the healing ceases and we may find ourselves slipping backward. I am told by many older men who I see as mentors and father figures in my life, that the work really never stops. We keep healing, evolving, growing, developing—or we stagnate. Maintaining these practices is what I can attribute my full healing and recovery to.

I have moved beyond abuse, and I have healed. You can too, and that is my desire and intention for you.

PART · TWO

The Spiritual Practices

AN INTRODUCION TO PART TWO

I think we can safely conclude that most people have an awareness of the divisiveness in our world related to our perceptions over differences between religions and their related spiritual practices. In my opinion, we become misguided when we form a conclusion that it is our specific practice, religion, or brand of spirituality that achieves the best response or results in a superior connection with the Divine. I am also of the opinion that God is not responding to the specific spiritual practices or religious traditions we engage in. Rather, I believe God responds to each of us individually in accordance with our own belief and faith. The practices and religious traditions simply exist to create faith within us. The practices are the tools, the means, and the methods we use to experience the Divine and all that comes with It.

We need to find the practices best suited to each of us to create and sustain a sense of faith within ourselves. We also need to allow others to discover which practices best suit them in developing and growing their own faith. We need to rid ourselves of false ideas of Divine favoritism for one particular practice, path, or religious tradition. There would be far less conflict, war, and fighting in the world if people would come to this realization and stop fighting over whose practices, traditions, or dogma is best suited to contact and maintain a relationship with God. If a particular practice succeeds at developing faith within an individual, and it does not harm or take any good away from anyone else, I believe it is a worthy practice and one of the infinite pathways to establish faith, to form a relationship with God, and to heal from traumatic experiences.

I chose to include the practices described in the subsequent chapters only because they worked for me to achieve my goals of healing. There are countless spiritual practices and traditions in the world, and all of them could probably be used in some way to facilitate healing from abusive experiences. The ones I include here simply worked well for me. I certainly do not believe these are necessarily the best or the only practices we can use to facilitate healing from childhood abuse.

I hope readers find some benefit in experimenting with the practices I include here. Mostly, I hope readers have the ambition to discover and implement the unique form and combination of spiritual practices that best support your own process of healing.

My most important piece of advice: Find the practice(s) that resonate with you and provide you the most benefit, then use them to heal and grow.

CHAPTER • 7

Meditation

In my own healing journey, I found meditation to be the most important and necessary spiritual practice to implement and maintain in order to achieve lasting healing from the effects of my own abusive experiences. It was the cornerstone and the pillar I needed to have in place before any of the subsequent practices I used could be effective.

I address two topics in this chapter. The first is how to meditate. What exactly is meditation, what are we doing, what are we experiencing, and what does it feel like? How do we deliberately put ourselves into a state of altered consciousness characterized by theta brain wave activity? How do we know when we are in this state, and how do we get there?

The second topic is the use of meditation to start healing the lasting effects of abusive experiences. Once we achieve a state of deep meditation and can do so on a regular basis, then what do we do with it? How do we actually dig into our subconscious minds and expose, uproot, and heal our emotional baggage derived from our abusive experiences? The aspects I cover on both of these topics are derived from my own personal experiences using meditation as a daily practice for the past six years. I also describe the processes and techniques that worked for me to dig up and heal my own emotional baggage.

The lasting effects from experiences of prolonged abuse become buried in our subconscious minds. The addictions, the habitual reactive behaviors, and the undesirable patterns we engage in, whether in our careers or our relationships, are the superficial manifestations of what is going on underneath. What is truly operating behind these outward patterns is pain, emotional trauma, fear, and limiting core beliefs about ourselves and others. All of these have typically been buried deeply and repressed, and I will refer to all of this collectively as "emotional baggage." To heal this baggage and change these outward manifestations operating in our lives, we have to access our subconscious minds; and we have to dig up, expose, and uproot these things. Meditation is a spiritual practice allowing us to access our subconscious minds and do this work.

In his book *Breaking the Habit of Being Yourself,* Dr. Joe Dispenza provides a significant amount of information on the relationship between our central nervous system, brain activity, and meditation. He writes that the brain primarily produces four distinct signals or types of electromagnetic activity in most adults: beta, alpha, theta, and delta waves. These states of electromagnetic activity in the brain correspond with whatever type of activity we engage in.

Beta waves are dominant when we are in alert and attentive states, and they are further subdivided into high, medium, and low ranges. High beta waves are produced when we are in a state of stress, and low beta waves are produced when we are in an attentive, yet relaxed state. Alpha waves occur when we are awake but in a relaxed state and focused more on our own thoughts than on taking in external sensory information. Theta waves dominate when we are in what he describes as a lucid state: Our bodies are asleep, but our minds are awake. Dispenza explains in his book that when our brains are in the theta state, we can access our subconscious mind, and this technique is used extensively in hypnotherapy. Delta waves dominate when we are in deep sleep.

Dispenza says that when we are in the theta state, the electromagnetic activity produced by our brain is coherent, ordered, and synchronized. Deep meditation that initiates the theta state is calming and relaxing, and it has been found to have tremendous benefits on brain function and overall health. In deep meditation, we can detach from our thoughts, our emotions, our bodies, our sensory perceptions, and even our physical environment. However, when we enter this state, we can still feel an awareness present and operating, and we can consciously use it. Once immersed in this state of awareness, we can deliberately use this awareness to focus on, tune into, and feel any part of our bodies. We can use it to truly feel any emotions we experience in the present moment or that we have experienced in our past. Most relevant to healing the effects of abuse, it is in this altered state of consciousness that we can use this awareness to deliberately dig up and expose emotional baggage stored within our subconscious minds.

My Experience with Meditation

So what exactly is meditation, and what are we doing when we meditate? Meditation is essentially getting ourselves into a state in which we are no longer thinking. In *The Power of Now,*

Eckhart Tolle describes an individual he observes in public talking out loud to himself. He discusses that most of us have encountered such individuals at one point or another in our lives, and we may have a tendency to label them as mentally ill or perhaps even insane. But the reality is, as he points out, we all do this all the time. The only difference between the person we label as mentally ill and us is that they are doing it out loud, while the rest of us do it inside our own heads.

There is a voice (or many voices) inside each of our minds, prattling away almost constantly throughout the day as we process sensory information, have our experiences, and go through our tasks. This voice constantly judges, analyzes, interprets, plans the future, brings up the past, replays experiences and emotions, and so on. It is the ongoing and unceasing activity of our minds. In his book, Tolle discusses the importance of being present, and one of the techniques he describes to attain this state is to start observing or listening to this activity going on in our minds.

When we implement this technique, an amazing thing happens. The voice shuts off, or rather we stop thinking for a brief moment. The longer and more often we practice this, the longer the stretches last when we are not thinking and are truly present. You can practice this technique right now by putting down this book and taking a few moments to begin observing and listening to your own thoughts. See if you successfully stop the thinking and pay attention to what this feels like.

Meditation is a technique or a practice used to shut off this voice, to turn off our mind's activity, and to stop thinking entirely for long periods of time. It is shifting ourselves from a thinking and analyzing state into a feeling state, in which we are not thinking at all. So how do we get there? Before I started a meditation practice, I had no idea what it actually entailed. In my mind, I had a picture of an individual sitting in the lotus posture on a pillow with their eyes closed, possibly chanting "Om."

What I know now is the method we use to get ourselves into this state, in which these theta brain waves take over, is called an induction. Performing an induction can essentially be understood as a form of self-hypnosis. One of the benefits I find is there is no right or wrong way to do an induction. In fact, there may be infinite methods to achieve an induction, and I will cover several that work for me. I recommend trying several techniques to find what works best for you. You may find yourself experimenting with different induction techniques through time, as I have.

Induction Techniques

To achieve an induction, you generally should sit upright in a chair, legs uncrossed, with your feet flat on the floor. Or you can sit on a pillow or mat with your legs crossed. Your posture should be erect, with your spine straight and your eyes closed. Sitting in a straight-backed chair or sitting with your back against a wall if you are using a pillow or cushion helps keep your back straight. I have found if I lie down or slouch, I am more likely to fall asleep. Standing up makes it more difficult for me to concentrate, though later I will discuss various activities not performed in seated positions that can be used to begin/assist with an induction. Your physical environment needs to be free of distractions, and your time needs to be uninterrupted.

One common thread that seems to be necessary with any induction technique is breath control. This activity involves bringing our conscious awareness to our breath and controlling the rhythm of our breathing. Breath control alone can be used to accomplish an induction, or it can be supplemented with other forms of concentration. Breath control and focusing our awareness fully on our breath is mentioned in every piece of New Thought or Science of Mind literature I have read that discusses meditation. Most guided meditations I have attended in workshops or classes have included some aspect of breath control and awareness of our breath at the beginning. I also subscribe to lessons through the Self-Realization Fellowship founded by Paramahansa Yogananda (an organization that emphasizes meditation as a means to discover and connect with God within yourself). The methods they teach for induction also involve breath control. I currently use their practices on a regular basis for my meditations.

Breath control requires you to focus your attention or your awareness fully on your breathing. Focusing solely on the sensations occurring in our bodies while we are breathing results in a cessation of thinking. It is a useful biological trick we can use to turn off our minds at will and cause our brains to move into the theta wave state. The longer you can maintain your attention on your breathing without thinking, the more relaxed you become, and with time you automatically shift into a deep meditative state. Deep breathing is not entirely necessary, but it does have a way of relaxing the body and the mind, and it is also proven to lower the heart rate and blood pressure.

I recommend to anyone just beginning a meditation practice to implement deep breathing, as it helps to keep your attention focused on your breath.

Essentially, you want to take long, slow, deep inhalations and attempt to completely fill your lungs with air. Complete the entire inhalation through your nose. You can experiment with pausing after completing the inhale and try holding your breath for a few moments, but do it without straining or causing any discomfort. Then similarly, engage in a long, slow, and controlled exhale out through your mouth and release all of the air from the lungs. You want to continue your exhale fully until there is a sensation that your lungs have been completely emptied of air.

During each breath, you want to maintain your full attention and awareness on your breathing. Focus completely on how it feels as air enters your nose. *Feel* your chest and abdomen expand during each inhalation. *Feel* the sensation as air exits your throat and mouth during the exhale. *Feel* your chest and abdomen contract during the exhale. Maintain all of your attention on these sensations in your body and on your rate of breathing.

If you notice your mind disengages and wanders to random thinking, gently pull it back and reengage your focus on your breathing and on the sensations occurring in your body related to your breathing. Pull your mind away from random thinking without judging or criticizing yourself. Beginners will notice their minds wanting to wander quite often, and it takes practice to refocus your attention on your breathing. It is important to remain completely still during this process and not move any parts of your body other than your chest and abdomen. You may notice an itch on your skin or an urge to shift or move due to cramps or discomfort. Try to ignore these sensations and dismiss them. These urges will pass with time and practice.

After you maintain this process for ten to fifteen minutes—fully keeping your awareness on your breath, maintaining stillness in your body, pulling your attention away from random thoughts—your thoughts should stop completely. You should feel completely relaxed, almost in a state of sleep but with an awareness still present. If you maintain this practice on a daily basis for seven straight days and give it a full ten to fifteen minutes each time, being diligent about controlling your mind and body, you should be able to achieve a state of induction by the end of the seventh day.

Once you feel you are in a calm and peaceful state and you can recognize no thoughts are occurring, you can resume normal breathing. Continue to maintain your attention on your breathing. You should notice your breathing rate is much slower and shallower than it normally is when you are active. You may even notice you do not need to breathe at all for short moments between inhalations and exhalations. These brief moments without breathing are when you can truly feel the Presence and the Awareness within you.

There are many other induction techniques that have worked well for me once I started exploring a meditation practice. The common thread between the ones that worked best for me is that they involve a "feeling" aspect. For me, it seems when there is a deliberate shift made from thinking to focusing on how certain things feel and concentrating on and bringing my full attention to how they feel, the thoughts just automatically stop and my brain gradually shifts into a state of deep meditation.

When I first started exploring meditation, I tried several guided meditations that used visualizing techniques. These did not work for me initially. I could not get my mind to focus on or cooperate with sticking to the visualizations. Instead, my mind would start to wander to other things. At times, I felt like the visualizations that the guides were instructing me to do were just too complex for my mind to hold onto. For me, visualizing becomes easier *after* I achieve an induction and enter into a meditative state.

The first time I successfully performed an induction and entered a deep meditation was through a guided process in which the guide had us focus on *feeling* various parts of the body. This individual operated his own life coaching business, where he taught meditation practices, among many other things. Initially, we used breath control and focused on the breath and the sensations that occurred in the body while breathing, as I describe above. He then had us focus our attention individually on our seven energy centers or chakras. Biologically, these energy centers are understood as regions in our body where major nerve branches connect with the spinal cord or where there is heightened activity in our central nervous systems to keep our bodies functioning.

Another guided meditation that worked successfully for me is provided on Dr. Joe Dispenza's website and is called "The Body Parts—Space Meditation" (https://drjoedispenza.com/products/body-parts-space-meditation-for-breaking-the-habit-of-being-yourself-updated-version-by-dr-joe-dispenza-meditation). This guided meditation is supplemental material for his book *Breaking the Habit of Being Yourself*, and it worked well for me to achieve an induction. After an exercise of breath control, Dizpenza guides you to bring your awareness to individual body parts and focus your full attention on them and how they feel. He has you hold your attention on a particular body part for a period of time before shifting your awareness to a new one. This technique was developed and has been extensively taught by Eastern religious traditions for centuries and is referred to as *Yoga Nidra*. Guided sessions by others can also be found through an internet search.

Another induction technique I have used successfully is taught through the Self-Realization Fellowship lessons I mentioned earlier. Using this technique, you bring your awareness to various muscle groups in your body, tensing and relaxing them in a specific order. Similar to Dispenza's method, this technique is also preceded by a breath control exercise, and it involves concentration on feeling the sensations in various body parts.

What these methods have in common is a focus on *feeling* different parts of your body. I am going to refer to these methods collectively as "body part inductions." Essentially, all that is required is bringing your full attention and awareness to different parts of your body and focusing all of your attention on how they feel—not thinking about the body parts, but truly feeling them. This is typically performed after a controlled breathing exercise, and I believe it is more successful if conducted in this order. To get a sense for this, stop reading at the end of this paragraph, then close your eyes and feel your hands and fingers. Focus on how the book and pages feel in your hands and in your fingers. Try to bring your attention to various parts of your hands individually and spend a few seconds feeling your fingertips, your individual digits one at a time, your knuckles, your palms, the backs of your hands, then perhaps the entirety of both of your hands. Do this for a couple of minutes and notice if you stop thinking.

In a body part induction, the particular order you choose to progress in focusing your attention on each body part does not seem to matter much, with exception of maintaining a top-down (head to toes) or bottom-up (toes to head) approach. If the chakras are the body parts you want to focus on, the guided meditations I am familiar with ask participants to start at the base of the spine and work their way up the seven chakras in order, ending with the crown chakra at the top of the head.

To achieve an induction using a body part technique, you must truly focus your full attention on each body part individually for at least one to two minutes. Similar to the breath control, if you catch your focus drifting away and notice your mind creating thoughts, bring it back to focusing and feeling whatever body part you left off with. These techniques, or any you can create on your own, seem to be an effective method to shift the brain and body from a thinking state into a feeling state, which results in the brain moving into a theta wave activity pattern.

Other induction techniques I have successfully used involve sound or vibration. But again, the goal is not to think about or try to analyze the sounds. Rather, the goal is to be fully active in just listening to and trying to feel the sounds in the body. Sound is nothing more than a vibration, and we have the ability to feel the vibration on or within our bodies, if we concentrate on it. The types of sounds that work best for me involve long, single-toned vibrations or a repetitive, monotonous beat via drumming. Vibrational sounds can be produced by Tibetan singing bowls, chimes, bells, and gongs. I once attended a gong bath, where the participants laid on the ground with their heads pointed toward four full-sized gongs, while two professionals trained in this type of meditation practice played the gongs and produced a wide variety of sounds and vibrations. For me, this experience can best be described as meditation on steroids.

Chanting is another induction technique I was introduced to in a guided setting that also worked well. This technique is similar to using the sounds mentioned above. I attended a session guided by a Qigong master, who had us repeatedly produce single-syllable and single-toned chants for the entirety of long, deep exhalations. At the same time we were producing this sound, he had us focus our attention on a particular region in the body.

A similar practice can be used while chanting single-syllable sounds originating from Sanskrit. Each chakra has a single-syllable chant associated with it that can be used while focusing one's attention on the respective chakra. Similarly, the goal in this exercise is to feel the vibration within your body as you produce the sound.

Listening to natural sounds is another technique I use to achieve an induction. Birds singing, water flowing (even artificially with a fountain), the rhythmic sound of ocean waves, the sound of a breeze rustling through the branches and leaves of trees, or even the random cacophony produced by a multitude of insects and animals in a rainforest have helped me achieve an induction. Such recorded sounds are available on CDs or online, and are specifically intended for meditation. I have also found many guided meditations using sounds from nature as a backdrop to their process.

In addition to these techniques, I also use more active methods to help bring on an induction, but for me these still require me to still my body and return to breath control following the activity. I have achieved an induction while standing, focusing on breath control, and slowly rocking back and forth on both feet while holding my attention on my legs and the feeling of alternating pressure at the bottoms of my feet. I also know many individuals who achieve inductions by mindfully and attentively walking a labyrinth.

Yoga is a form of exercise lending itself to holding particular poses or stretches, requiring full attention be given to the engaged body parts. This practice is similar to a body part induction, but it introduces slow and controlled movement into the technique. The type of yoga that works best for this is not the fast-paced aerobic style, but rather the type requiring you to slowly transition from one pose to another with controlled movement while holding each pose for several seconds. Vinyasa, Iyengar, and Kundalini are examples. I find I can quickly produce an induction within just a couple of minutes following this type of yoga session, once I still my body and engage my attention on controlled breathing.

Recognizing the Induction State

So how do you know if you have successfully achieved an induction? What does it feel like? What happens? The best way

I can describe this is by sharing what occurs with me and what others who engage in regular meditation have communicated to me.

After successfully completing an induction and entering into a state of deep meditation, you should not have any thoughts occurring. The constant prattling and noise made by the mind during our normal awakened state should be silent. You can literally bring your awareness and attention to the center of your head, and there should be nothing going on there except an awareness and a feeling of a peaceful presence. If a car goes by or a dog barks, you might hear it, but you have no thoughts about it. You should also be able to successfully shift your awareness around to various parts or regions of your body, or to focus on feeling your entire body at once without thinking.

It is almost a state of being asleep, though you are not tired or dreaming. If you start dreaming, bring your focus back to your breath or body parts. This is an indication you are shifting into delta wave brain activity and falling asleep. If this happens repeatedly when you attempt to meditate, you likely are not getting enough sleep. I ran into this problem and found taking a twenty-to-thirty-minute power nap prior to meditation allowed me to achieve an induction without slipping into a sleep state.

Another sign you have successfully achieved an induction, is if you bring your awareness to any particular part of your body and leave it there, you should not feel any other part of your body. Once I achieve an induction, I typically bring my awareness either to the center of my head (the third eye chakra) or to my heart center and leave it there. With time, I lose all sensation or feeling from the rest of my body. I do not feel my feet on the floor. I do not feel the pressure of the chair on my bottom any longer. All sensation of touch, temperature, or pressure is completely gone. There is almost a feeling of paralysis, but I do not have any desire to move. It is so relaxing, I have a strong preference to remain in this state. Ultimately, I lose all perception of feeling anything in my body, and I at times experience a sensation of weightlessness.

This can be referred to as an out-of-body experience, and I have spoken with many individuals who regularly engage in meditation who have experienced these sensations. Some experience a sense of actually leaving their bodies. Others, myself included, experience a sensation of getting smaller and smaller and going deeper and deeper within our bodies or perhaps into our hearts, heads, or minds. This is difficult to explain; it is something you have to feel and experience on your own in order to understand. All I can say is you will know it when you experience it.

A deep meditation produces a deep and profound sense of peace, calm, and serenity, along with other potential feelings of intense joy, love, and bliss. I often feel energy coursing through my body that feels like goose bumps before I completely detach from bodily sensations. If you focus your awareness on your third eye chakra, you may perceive lights or colors even though your eyes are closed and you may be in a darkened room.

Another sensation that sometimes occurs to me during deep meditation is a complete loss of my sense of time. I have performed two- to three-hour-long meditations on occasion that seemed to go by in an instant. The experience is similar to being placed under anesthesia and then waking up after a surgery: There is no concept of time elapsing. However, in meditation you still maintain consciousness and awareness. This awareness and the positive energy emanating from it is your soul, your spirit, your unique connection with an expression of the Divine. We all contain this within us, and it is who and what we truly are. Meditation allows us to access it, connect with it, and feel it.

Another sign you have achieved an induction and entered deep meditation is, once you choose to wake up or bring your sensory awareness back, you may sometimes find it difficult or it may seem to take conscious effort to begin feeling or moving various parts of your body again. There may be tingling sensations in your extremities or in your arms and legs. When you open your eyes and start seeing again for the first time, things just appear different—there is more color, there is more light, and everything just looks more vibrant and amazing. It may be difficult to stand or walk right away. Trying to do something complex, like driving a vehicle, right away is certainly not a good idea.

Just as it takes time for the brain to transition into a theta wave state, it also takes time to transition back to a wakeful and alert beta wave state, sometimes longer than it takes when you first wake up from deep sleep. Similar to the sensation of paralysis I describe above, there will be a preference to not move and to remain in this relaxed and calm state. You will find that feeling and movement will return to your body gradually and at a natural pace that comes on its own.

How to Use Meditation for Healing

Once we successfully achieve an induction and can enter into meditation on a regular basis, how do we use this practice to begin healing the effects of abuse? How do we deliberately go into the subconscious mind and dig up the emotional baggage, the buried emotional trauma, the fears, and the limiting core beliefs about ourselves? And how do we heal these?

I used a process of visualization, combined with focusing on feeling my emotions, to access my subconscious. This may sound like thinking, but it is different. The thinking we are doing in an alert beta wave state is much different from the visualizing we can accomplish once in a theta wave state. This type of visualization is a deliberate form of concentration, but it does not require the level of effort needed to sustain as concentrating in the beta wave state demands. The important part is to begin this visualization process *after* achieving an induction.

As an example, set this book down at the end of this sentence, and try to visualize a flower in your mind and to sustain the image for as long as possible. Most of us do not have the mental capacity to do this continuously in a beta wave state for longer than a minute or two before our minds start to wander to other things or to other thoughts. However, once in the theta wave state, you can deliberately bring forth a flower into your consciousness and keep it there for a considerable length of time. Sensory information about the flower is heightened: You may be able to actually smell it, you can certainly picture it clearly, and you may even choose to feel it. You may feel emotions rise up within you as you regard the flower from this state of full presence, emotions such as gratitude, appreciation, or a sense of awe and wonder. In a theta state, it is much easier to focus all of your attention and awareness on the flower (or onto anything else), and there is not much effort involved in maintaining your focus on this visualization. As we are in a state of feeling rather than thinking, emotions also become much clearer, both to feel and to discern.

What we are going to do in mediation to address the effects of abuse, once we achieve the theta brain wave state, is we are then going to deliberately visualize events and experiences when we felt those strong emotional reactions or responses we subsequently buried. Bringing these things up from the subconscious mind is what allows them to be healed. We are going to bring our full attention and awareness to how these experiences *feel*, and what the emotions *feel* like as they are coming forth in our bodies. Because we are doing this from a state of connection with our higher self and in full presence, healing energy, love, compassion, and light are automatically transmitted to these painful places, and healing takes place. We are also going to deliberately transfer healing energy and love into these experiences to enhance the healing process.

In one of the classes I attended through Centers for Spiritual Living, Existential Metapsychiatry, we learned that thoughts precede emotional reactions. Existential Metapsychiatry covered many topics, but the theme of this particular class was angerless living. We were exposed to the concept that there is always a thought occurring first in our minds, which then leads to the experience or reaction of anger. Identifying these thoughts and consciously changing them assists us in moving through our lives with less and less anger toward the circumstances, experiences, or people who harmed us.

When it comes to using meditation for healing the effects of abuse and digging into our subconscious minds to unearth emotional baggage, a similar process is operating—but in reverse. When we experienced abusive events and other trauma back in our childhoods, our minds quickly created thoughts and beliefs about ourselves and about the events. Extremely painful emotions also arose. Our brains and bodies are wired to avoid pain as a survival mechanism, so we learned to suppress or stuff these emotions down when they arose instead of allowing them to be fully expressed. Also, we may have lived in an environment where we were afraid to express our emotions, or where it may not have been safe for us to do so. The thoughts and beliefs associated with those repressed emotions were also stuffed down and retained within us. These repressed emotions, thoughts, and beliefs have a tendency to linger and play out in our lives until we allow them to be fully expressed and understood. They also remain within us until we uproot them and change them.

Using meditation to identify and expose the false thoughts or limiting beliefs buried in our subconscious requires us to *feel* the emotions first. The thoughts and beliefs are buried and hidden, but the emotions are right there front and center in our day-to-day lives. This is the reverse process I speak of: We cannot identify the buried thoughts or beliefs until we allow ourselves to fully feel the emotions first.

While in a state of deep meditation, in full presence, and immersed completely in the awareness within each of us, we must shift and focus our attention completely into these emotions and allow ourselves to completely and fully *feel* them. When we do this and become fully present to how they *feel*, the thoughts or beliefs hidden behind the emotions surface and become apparent on their own. Once we identify and expose these thoughts and beliefs, we can then uproot them, heal them, and change them. We do this through prayer and spiritual mind treatment, which I discuss in the next chapter.

The question then becomes how we discern whether an emotion we experience is just a fleeting, temporary emotional reaction/response versus an emotional state related to our baggage. Answering this question requires us to be completely honest and authentic with ourselves. It is those emotional states or emotional reactions you experience on a repetitive and recurring basis that are related to buried thoughts and beliefs in your subconscious. It is necessary to recognize and become familiar with these repetitive emotional states. Doing so will allow you to bring them forth and feel them without effort during a meditation.

These repetitive emotional states, for me, revolved around feelings of resentment, feelings of defensiveness, the way I felt when I criticized or judged someone or myself, feelings of loneliness, the way I felt when I craved sugar or sweets, and the way I felt when the urges came to find sex, seek out a romantic relationship, or masturbate excessively to deal with stress. All of these emotional states were repetitive themes in my life. The specific characteristics of how I felt with each theme were unique, and I also experienced them all repetitively. Allowing myself to completely feel these emotions in a deep meditative state ultimately brought forth the buried false thoughts or limiting beliefs that existed behind the emotions. These buried thoughts or beliefs became clear on their own through my intuition when I allowed myself to be present with each emotional state. I also found many of the emotions and false thoughts or beliefs were related or connected to one another.

I emphasize the word *feel* to describe this process because it is critical to understand this is an exercise of feeling. This is not an exercise of thinking, judging, or analyzing. The instant we find ourselves thinking about, judging, or analyzing the emotions or memories, we are no longer in a state of meditation. We need to be in a *feeling* state and to be fully present to how these emotional states *feel* in our bodies.

There are two methods we can use to bring this feeling state into a meditation through the visualization process I describe above. The first is to become present to one of these emotional conditions in the moment and at a time when we are experiencing that particular condition (following the termination of a job, at the ending of a significant relationship, following a habitual angry outburst or emotional reaction, etc.). The second method is to artificially bring forth the emotion by bringing our awareness to a past experience when we strongly felt it and to then visualize the past experience.

Once either of these methods is implemented in meditation and we bring our full awareness to how the emotional condition feels, we then continue with the visualization process and allow additional experiences to come forth from times when we felt this same emotional condition. During this process, we must keep our awareness focused on how this emotional condition feels as we replay these scenes from our lives like a movie reel. Because you are accessing your subconscious mind through deep mediation, the experiences should come forth on their own and with little effort. There is no need to strain or to attempt to force the memories to come forth. For me, they came forward one after another, after another, after another as I sat and remained fully present with the feeling of the particular emotional state. The scenes played out on their own like a movie reel, without any effort on my part to dig them up. I simply had to sit and feel.

The goal is to watch and listen to the scenes and to be fully present to how the emotions feel in our minds and in our bodies. This process allowed me to identify the limiting thoughts or beliefs behind my own emotional trauma. If it did not come immediately to me in the meditation, it often came a short time later in dreams, while journaling, or in a sudden intuitive hit when I was focused on the memories in an awakened state. In some way, though, the limiting thoughts or beliefs behind these emotions always came through.

For individuals who have experienced abuse and significant trauma, this work is extremely difficult because it is extremely painful. When you do this, you call forth and bring up deeply buried emotional pain related to your traumatic experiences. The pain can seem excruciating, but allowing it to come forth and flow out of you is what allows you to heal it. When I did this work, I experienced intense emotional reactions that left me weeping intensely for long durations of time, particularly when I explored my resentment and my fears of loneliness. At times, the emotional reactions were accompanied by physical symptoms, such as pain in my chest or heart, discomfort in my digestive tract, muscle cramps, headaches, or tension elsewhere in my body.

In these meditations, I sat and watched as I was beaten and thrown around like a rag doll by my father. I felt his hands under my armpits and felt his terrifying physical strength directed at hurting me as he slammed me into walls or through closets in my parents' home. I felt him pummeling my face and head with his open hands, and I stared into the uncontrolled rage that distorted his face. I felt him paddling me relentlessly to the point of where I could not stand up, and I cried my eyes dry over the pain and humiliation. I listened to him demean me and make fun of me, curse at me, and scream at me. I fully felt my own anger, terror, and resentment toward him.

I sat and witnessed my mother exploding into a temper and felt her slapping me repeatedly in the face. I watched the lightning spark in her eyes as she reacted toward me in her rage. I fully felt the frustration and pain over not being permitted to speak my mind or express my thoughts, emotions, or feelings to her or to my father. I fully felt the humiliation and worthlessness I adopted from these experiences. I experienced all of the fear, pain, anger, hatred, resentment, disappointment, frustration, loneliness, isolation, and desperation —fully and completely. This process was brutal; it was excruciating; and the pain I felt while doing this was at times crippling and debilitating.

However, almost in the same moments when I was fully feeling all of the pain associated with these traumatic experiences and just allowing the pain to flow and allowing myself to cry, I also felt healing energy come and fill the space left by pulling out these deeply rooted emotions. That healing presence, that energy, that love, kindness, and compassion comes in on its own. It comes in at the same instant you are shedding tears from the pain. Then the tears begin to flow with a sense of joy rather than sadness as you are filled with peace, love, bliss, and gratitude. The only way I can explain this sensation is it is a warmth, a presence, a loving energy, and a deep sense of care and compassion that takes over and completely dissolves every aspect of those painful experiences. It completely fills you, overwhelms you, and releases you from the burden of your pain. It is something you will know and recognize once you feel it and experience it. It is, purely and simply, a deep sense of true and profound peace, love, and healing.

I also learned you can bring in this peaceful and loving energy deliberately through the same visualization process. You watch yourself as you are being beaten and broken as a child or as an adult. You see yourself as you go through these experiences. You listen as you are degraded and torn down with obscenities, shouting, and cruelty. And you feel every part of it. Then you come between your child self and the offender, and you gently push the offender away. Your power and awareness blocks them and stops them completely in their actions. Their negative, angry, and hateful energy cannot penetrate or pass through this power within you. They become paralyzed, mute, and completely powerless. Then you approach that broken, crying, and sobbing child or adult lying on the floor, and you pick them up. You hold them close. You comfort them, console them, and send them love and compassion. You wipe away their tears. You stroke their head and their back. You hug them tightly, and you reassure them that they are loved unconditionally and fully accepted in all ways. You fill them with reassuring, affirmative, and compassionate words of love and kindness.

I found these to be effective methods to confront and heal my emotional baggage when I used them as a regular practice of meditation. I stand firm in my statement: This works, and it results in tremendous healing and growth. Your self-awareness and your awareness of your higher self become more and more pronounced every time you do these exercises.

You may wonder, when do you stop? How long or how many times does this take? How do you know when you have healed the emotional baggage? As I stated above, the limiting thoughts, fears, or core beliefs buried behind these emotions will come forth on their own. Having the awareness of these operating in your life is in itself a sign that healing is occurring. I personally implemented this practice to individually attack every repetitive undesirable emotional condition I was able to identify. For each and every one of these conditions, I was able to go back in time and see myself experiencing the conditions over and over again, all the way back until I was a small child. I found it fascinating and enlightening.

For me, it always took more than a single meditation session to tackle a particular condition. I knew I was healed when I could visualize experiences once related to a condition and when I no longer felt any emotional response or reaction within my body. Once I was healed, visualizing the experiences resulted in a neutral reaction or response in my mind and in my body. With time, visualizing the experiences even produced a response of joy and gratitude, because I recognized the healing and growth that occurred as a result of doing this work.

The other outward sign of healing is all the habits and behaviors once associated with buried trauma start to fall away and become easier to shed. Over time in doing this work, you feel lighter, happier, more peaceful, and your life will start to change for the better.

I recommend you set aside time for yourself to implement this practice for the more difficult experiences or emotions, and that you do so on open days without activities planned. In other words, it is probably not a good idea to dive into the emotions associated with extremely traumatic and abusive experiences on the same morning as a job interview. You should set aside at least a half day or even a full day to give yourself the rest, care, and compassion needed to decompress from these exercises. I found taking naps to be beneficial. They seemed to provide a reset for my brain, nervous system, and body. My primary recommendation is to take care of and love yourself while you do this work.

I was able to do this work on my own, and I was able to complete it for the most part alone. This may not be true for some individuals, though, especially those who experienced a greater degree of trauma for more prolonged time periods than I. A close friend who is a psychiatrist commended me for being able to do this work on my own. But he cautioned me that some individuals may not be ready or be capable of digging into their own buried traumatic memories without risk of sliding into depression, suffering panic attacks, or backsliding into deeply engrained addictions or other self-destructive behaviors. Some individuals may need to practice these exercises within a controlled environment with a trained therapist, counselor, psychiatrist, psychologist, or spiritual practitioner. Desiring or needing the support or coaching of a trained individual to assist with your healing does not imply weakness. Rather, it demonstrates wisdom, strength, and deep intuition on your part. I encourage you to gauge your own level of comfort in taking on these exercises and this type of work and to make a conscious decision whether you feel you can take on these practices alone or whether you need the support and coaching of a trained professional or a loving partner.

This process is not easy, and this is why I refer to it as work. It requires regular practice, and I found I had to be careful in how I dosed myself so I would not become overwhelmed. I would often come out of these meditations feeling fatigued, as if I had just completed an intense physical workout. Any physical symptoms that arose in the meditations were always temporary, though, and they usually vanished if I allowed myself to rest or take a twenty- to thirty-minute power nap.

This work is difficult because the last thing our brains and our bodies want to do is call forth and bring up emotions and feel things associated with trauma. I can speak to this personally. There is resistance; there is reluctance; the body and the mind often do not want to cooperate. You will observe your mind starting to wander on its own to other things. Your body will want to fidget and be restless, or you may get distracted by itchy skin, a scratchy throat, muscle cramps, or any other variety of distractions that are your body's way of protecting itself from what you are about to subject it to.

The key is to practice and make repeated attempts. You have to learn to ignore your body and dismiss your mind when they begin to squirm while taking on this process. It is important to bring your attention back to the particular induction technique you are using to enter the meditative state. It is also important not to allow yourself to become frustrated and to refrain from judging or condemning yourself if your body or mind continually distract you. Engaging in this type of thinking will only sabotage your efforts. The goal is to dismiss these distractions from the body or the mind in a gentle and compassionate way. Allow the distractions to float by as a leaf being carried by a breeze across your living room window. Practice the induction techniques that work best for you over and over again until entering a meditative state becomes easy and natural for you.

The more you practice, the easier this becomes. And the more you practice, the more healing you experience. It is painful, but it is worth it. You and your life are also worth it.

CHAPTER • 8

Conscious Prayer

There is thinking, and there is prayer. I am learning more and more that there really is not much distinction between the two. Science of Mind teachings, both in the churches and in the literature, place a heavy emphasis on the power of our thoughts, and for a good reason. Our thoughts absolutely exhibit power, and they draw experiences and circumstances into our lives with both positive and negative effects. I have seen enough concrete evidence in my own life to convince me this principle is in constant operation. We also have the ability and choice to perceive circumstances, people, interactions, and events in either a positive or negative light, which is entirely dependent on our thinking about these things. In Science of Mind, we believe we are praying constantly with our thoughts and beliefs, whether we want to be or not. The trick is to take control of our thoughts, of our thinking, of our beliefs, and of the activity of our minds and to pray consciously or think consciously in alignment with the good we desire to have. Then we call more of it in.

What is the distinction between thinking and prayer? Is a fleeting, passing thought that skims across our mind for a split second a prayer? Are fanciful or whimsical thoughts prayers?

When another driver cuts you off or nearly sideswipes you on the highway because they are texting while driving, and you catch yourself having a quick vindictive thought about them, is that a prayer?

What Science of Mind teaches, and what I have come to learn through my own experience, is that thoughts—coupled with a strong intention, a strong conviction, a deep belief, and an absolute faith—constitute prayer. It is this type of thinking, coupled with strong emotion, that manifests tangible and relatable experiences or circumstances in our lives. We can try to think positive thoughts all day every day, but if the *belief* is not there, we likely will not experience significant changes. There is much concrete evidence and literature pointing to the fact that it is the repetitive and habitual thoughts, the more consistent patterns of thoughts or beliefs, that truly operate in the forefront of our lives.

Does a random thought constitute a prayer? Is there a direct response to each and every thought passing through our minds? I am not going to pretend to know the answer to this question. What I do know is that repetitive and habitual patterns of thinking, coupled with emotion, absolutely constitute prayer. I also know with certainty that there is a direct and unbiased response to the energy we release, bringing us circumstances that align with our habitual thinking and habitual emotions (i.e., our prayers). Whether our prayers are conducted consciously by us when we are in control of our minds or whether they are conducted unconsciously as we float around in life acting and reacting to circumstances, there is always an unbiased response, positive or negative. We are constantly drawing experiences and circumstances into our lives directly related to our deeply held core beliefs, our repetitive patterns of thought, and our habitual emotional reactions.

Once we progress in our meditation work and start unearthing our limiting core beliefs, habitual patterns of thinking, and repetitive emotional reactions operating as a result of abusive experiences, how do we change these? How do we heal them? Prayer, conscious prayer, is the answer. When we pull something out of our subconscious mind, heal it, and release it, then we need to replace it with something else. Repetitive thoughts of being no good, unlovable, unworthy, useless, or any other limitations we impose on ourselves—these false ideas have to be replaced if we wish to experience changes to our circumstances. We have to change our core beliefs about ourselves and replace the negative ones we uproot with positive ones to change our lives for the better. This is accomplished through conscious prayer.

I will not go into great detail of what exactly prayer is, what constitutes effective prayer, or how to pray with conscious intention or deliberate purpose. This work has already been completed by Ernest Holmes in his brilliant book *The Science of Mind.* I do not feel I can provide additional insight, nor can I provide further clarification as to what prayer is and how to pray effectively to achieve results as eloquently and with such clarity and conviction as Holmes achieved in this seminal work. I will, however, describe the basics and how I used these principles for my own healing.

The principles Holmes reveals in his work are the truth, and the methods he teaches for harnessing the power of God with effective prayer actually work. I used his methods to heal myself of all the effects from child abuse and domestic violence.

I completely changed and planted new core beliefs into my subconscious, and I am reaping the benefits of doing this work. Holmes states clearly in his book that readers should not just take what he says as absolute truth or fact. Rather, he encourages readers to experiment with these principles in their own lives and then watch the results occur for themselves. He provides us with a model, a technique, a method to use prayer effectively to bring concrete and tangible changes into our lives. An entire philosophy, a new way of thinking, a spiritual movement, and hundreds of churches and spiritual centers stem from his teachings. Those of us who are familiar with and practice Science of Mind principles often lovingly say to each other, "This stuff works!" because it really does.

I organized some quotes from Holmes's *The Science of Mind* that had a profound impact on the way I thought about or approached prayer, faith, and the action of God/Spirit in my life. Understanding these principles necessitated I completely change the ways in which I was habitually thinking.

> *We all know that many have been healed of physical disease through prayer. Let us analyze this. Why are some healed through prayer while others are not?... The answer is NOT that God has responded to some and not to others, but that some have responded to God more than others. ... The Universe is impersonal. It gives alike to all. It is no respecter of persons. It values each alike. ... Nothing could bring greater discouragement than to labor under the delusion that God is a Being of moods, who might answer SOME prayers and not others. There can be no God who is kindly disposed one day and cruel the next; there can be no God who creates us*

with tendencies and impulses we can scarcely comprehend, and then eternally punishes us when we make mistakes. God is a Universal Presence, an impersonal Observer, a Divine and impartial Giver.

Within us there is a creative field,... around us there is a creative field ... in reality they are One. There is one Mental Law in the Universe, and where we use It, It becomes our Law because we have individualized it. ... We must say that all thought is creative, according to the nature, impulse, emotion, or conviction behind the thought. Thought creates a mold ... and sets power in motion in accordance with the thought. Ignorance of this excuses no one from its effects, for we are dealing with Law. Experience has taught us that the subjective tendency of this intelligent Law of creative force may consciously be directed and definitely used. ... We need not ask why these things are so. ... We do not create laws and principles, but discover and make use of them. Let us accept this position relative to the laws of Mind and Spirit and see what we can do with them.

Our belief sets the limit to our demonstration of a Principle which, of Itself, is without limit. It is ready to fill everything, because It is Infinite. So, it is not a question of Its willingness, nor of Its ability. It is entirely a question of our own receptivity. ... It can pass into expression through us only as we consciously allow It to do so. ... It has been proved that by thinking correctly and by a conscious mental use of the Law of Mind, we can cause It to do definite things for us, through us. By conscious thinking, we give conscious direction to It, and It, consciously or unconsciously, responds to *our advance along the line of our conscious or subjective direction. It must and will respond to everyone, because it is Law and Law is no respecter of persons. ... This Law we did not create; this Law we cannot change. We can use It correctly only as we understand and use It according to Its nature.*

We should bear in mind that the prayers which are effective—no matter whose prayers they may be—are effective because they embody certain universal principles which, when understood, can be consciously used. IF GOD EVER ANSWERED A PRAYER, HE ALWAYS ANSWERS PRAYER. Prayer is not an act of overcoming God's reluctance, but should be an ACTIVE acceptance of His highest willingness. ... The possibility of further human evolution works through man's imagination and will. The time is now; the place is where we are; and it is done unto us as we believe.

What Holmes is stating here, and what he brings to light with such clarity in *The Science of Mind*, is that there is a universal principle that is but one characteristic or aspect of God operating on our behalf by making a direct response to our beliefs. He refers to this as the law, and we can use it consciously to draw in our own good, or we can use it unconsciously and draw in unpleasant experiences. It is unbiased and acts in accordance with our beliefs to bring us circumstances and experiences in alignment with what we believe—our beliefs being composed of our habitual modes of thinking coupled with repetitive emotional reactions.

Those of us who experienced abuse, particularly as children, carry very limiting core beliefs about ourselves within our subconscious minds. Once we identify them, we need only to look at our life experiences—choices around relationships, careers, friendships, family interactions, health, and repetitive habits—to see these limiting beliefs playing out on a grand scale. We can also discern quite clearly how we draw in or attract repetitive and similar experiences to our lives to reinforce these beliefs. This is the law in action, and it is demonstrating itself front and center in our experience for us to see and bear witness to.

We only need to take responsibility for our habitual patterns of thinking and our beliefs—and then change them—to draw more positive experiences into our lives. We only need to begin to use the law consciously and correctly. It is our responsibility to do so, and the only barriers we encounter to living a full and blessed life are those that were imposed on us and that we still choose to carry around within us. Once we make the choice to think differently, to change our beliefs about ourselves for the better, our life circumstances begin to change for the better. Science of Mind fanatics like myself particularly enjoy Holmes's catchy phrase, "Change your thinking, change your life."

The universal principles Holmes refers to that result in clear and undeniable demonstrations of our prayers have been adopted, studied, and taught by Centers for Spiritual Living institutions worldwide for the past ninety-plus years. This particular method of prayer is referred to as spiritual mind treatment, and I used this method to facilitate my own healing. Spiritual mind treatment comprises six distinct steps used to help us create the belief, the conviction, and the emotion necessary to accomplish concrete demonstrations for whatever it is we are praying for. It is done unto us in accordance with our belief, so our mission is to change the beliefs operating in our subconscious into more positive beliefs in alignment with the truth of who and what we are.

Step One: PURPOSE

The first step in a spiritual mind treatment is to determine and declare the purpose for giving the treatment. First, we must bring our awareness to the condition in our life (and the false belief behind the condition) that we wish to change. The condition is the outward manifestation of the false belief. An example present in my life: I was continually remaining involved in unhealthy and unfulfilling romantic relationships, often characterized by neglect and even abuse or violence. So the purpose of my treatments was stated as follows:

> *I am surrounded by kind, loving, compassionate, understanding, accepting, and supportive individuals. My relationships and my friendships are healthy, nurturing, and beneficial to my physical, emotional, and spiritual well-being.*

What is important in this step, and in the subsequent steps, is to speak or affirm in the present tense. It is critical to declare ownership of the manifestation or demonstration you wish to make *right now*. This helps create the mindset, the conviction, the belief, and the faith necessary to achieve a demonstration.

Once you declare ownership of your purpose, the treatment then begins. What is important to understand in the treatment(s) is that we are not attacking the conditions, nor are we paying attention to them (e.g., my romantic relationships are neglectful or abusive; my partners are rarely present; I am lonely). Focusing on or dwelling on the conditions only results in a continuation of them. We must instead attack the false belief behind the condition. We are interested only in changing ourselves and changing the false beliefs operating in our own minds. In the example here, the particular belief operating behind this condition in my life was an overwhelming fear of loneliness and isolation, and there was a false belief that I *needed* to be involved with a female companion in a romantic setting to fix this. My treatment then attacks the false belief and the fear.

Step Two: RECOGNITION

The next step to begin a treatment is referred to as recognition. In this step, we bring our awareness completely and fully to the fact that God (or Spirit or Creator, whatever you choose to call It) is in everything, is a part of everything, and is everything. All life, all creation, all matter, all energy contain and operate with a perfect harmony and Divine Intelligence that is ever-sustaining and ever-evolving and changing. This is the truth of all creation, from the frantic activity of subatomic particles making up the matter we are surrounded by and created from, to the infinite and incomprehensible vastness of the entire universe. There is a Divine Intelligence and order operating within and as part of it all.

To see this, we only need to become present and aware of the vast amount of activity occurring in the atoms and molecules of even simple inanimate objects. We can concentrate on and appreciate the vast amount of complex activity occurring constantly within the cells, tissues, and organs of our bodies. We can focus on and ponder all the life and processes occurring in a natural setting as simple as our front yards, bringing our awareness to the countless bacteria and other organisms interacting, the variety and uniqueness of each blade of grass, and the infinite processes occurring constantly between the soil, water, air, plants, other living organisms, and sunlight. We can gaze at the heavens and the stars and attempt to comprehend just how vast the universe really is by observing the many stars we can see of our galaxy, understanding how far away they are and how large our galaxy is, and knowing there are billions, if not trillions, of other galaxies beyond ours. I do not believe it is possible to truly become present to the miracle of creation surrounding us constantly and not become aware of a Divine Presence operating. The continuous process of sustaining and evolving creation occurs around us constantly, and it also occurs within us constantly. All of this operates in perfect stillness, peace, and silence. When we bring our awareness to this and become present to it, we can *feel* a Divine Presence because we are part of it.

The goal in the recognition stage of a treatment is to ponder, meditate on, or concentrate on any or all aspects of creation or life to bring your awareness to this Divine Intelligence and harmony we refer to as God. For the remainder of the treatment to be effective, you must remain in or work with this recognition stage until you can truly *feel* and be aware of this Divine Presence within everything and operating everywhere. There is no right or wrong way to accomplish this. Each path or process taken is unique to the individual, and each individual must focus on, ponder, or think about whatever aspect of creation or life best brings this awareness front and center.

As an example for the recognition state, I offer this:

I recognize there is one infinite and universal power operating in and through every aspect of creation. It is continuously unfolding in beauty and harmony, expressing itself in every particle, every organism, every star and planet, and in the entirety of the universe. I recognize the vastness of this power, continuously unfolding in all places in the universe here and now and in all moments. It is an infinite and unconditional loving presence, containing the qualities of wisdom, intelligence, beauty, harmony, kindness, compassion—all things good and all energy beneficial.

Step Three: UNIFICATION

The next stage of a treatment is referred to as unification. In this stage, we accept and declare that because all creation is God, and we are a part of creation, we are also one with, intimately connected with, and a part of God. We bring our awareness to the fact that we are a unique and individual expression of God. We also bring our awareness to the interconnectedness of all of humanity and all of creation. Everything is connected, everything is of God, everything is one.

When we speak our prayers into this feeling, we open ourselves to infinite possibility through our connection with all of creation. When we recognize and truly feel this connection with God and realize our oneness with all of creation, we open ourselves to the action of Divine Intelligence. This same Intelligence orchestrates all of creation and keeps it operating in harmony. Therefore, we can trust It to align the circumstances, people, resources, and guidance necessary to bring about the manifestation we desire.

This stage of a treatment is deeply personal and unique from person to person. The same advice I gave above also holds true for this stage of a treatment: Hold your awareness and focus fully on the idea that not only are you a unique expression of God, but that you are also connected and one with God and with everything. Any form of concentration, meditation, words, ideas, or thoughts to bring forth this conviction and create the feeling of this interconnectedness will suffice. Similar to the previous step in beginning a treatment, there is no right or wrong way to accomplish this. The ultimate goal is to become fully aware of the feeling of divinity within you and your connection to all of creation and to God.

> *Knowing I am a unique part of creation, that the very essence of God that flows through every aspect of creation also flows through and expresses itself uniquely as me, I know I contain within me all of the qualities and energies of the Divine. This divine energy connects me and unites me with all of life and all of creation. It is all interconnected, all one. With this understanding, I know as I speak from this presence and source within me, as these words and intentions flow out into creation, I understand it is simply Spirit communing with Itself. Therefore, all things are possible, and Spirit is working on my behalf through every part of creation in response to my intentions and my faith.*

I achieve recognition and unification steps most effectively through meditation, then visualizing any scene or experience when I truly feel connected to God or to others. These initial steps of a treatment create the belief, the feeling, the faith, and the conviction necessary so the words we speak next to conduct our treatment carry with them a feeling, an emotion, and a deep essence of undeniable truth. This is the key to creating the belief within you, such that the phrase, "As you believe, it shall be done unto you," aligns with your particular treatment. These first steps should cast aside any doubt or uncertainty whatsoever in your mind and bring forth a state of deep faith and conviction that the treatment being given will indeed come to pass.

Step Four: REALIZATION

The next stage of a treatment is referred to as realization. Once we create the feeling of God in everything and our connection with God, we then state the truth for ourselves. In this stage, we affirm our highest good in alignment with what we desire, as stated in our purpose. In this stage of the treatment, it is important to make your declarations in the present tense. The manifestation occurs *right now;* there is an immediate and direct response to the prayer *right now*. As we speak our words during this stage of the treatment, it is crucial to hold the belief, the conviction, and the faith in a Power responding to our words and to our intentions.

Ernest Holmes describes two different methods for conducting this stage of a treatment. One method uses a process of logic and denial to renounce as false the conditions you wish to change. The other method is to affirm the opposite of the condition and speak only in alignment with the intentions you hold. I have experienced demonstrations using both methods.

Here is an example I used to attack the limiting beliefs or fears I held that resulted in calling in unhealthy or unfulfilling relationships:

> *I affirm right now in this moment, I am never alone. Any fears of isolation and loneliness dissolve and are removed from me the instant I recognize and connect with the truth of who and what I am. I am a unique and individual manifestation of the Divine. The same qualities of God, Spirit, and Source that created and sustain everything in the entire universe exist within me, now and always. Any energy or thoughts of lack or limitation are not compatible with this truth, and these false ideas fall away from me and are shed completely. They are dissolved as light dissolves the darkness; they are incinerated by the fire of the Source within me; they are washed away with the clean and pure water of Spirit.*
>
> *I know and fully accept as I move forth in life—holding the truth of what I am, as I carry the attributes of the Divine front and center in my experience—I am blessed with corresponding energy. I show up with kindness, compassion, understanding, acceptance, and love. I recognize the Divine in every person I encounter. With this recognition, I experience the oneness and interconnectedness of us all. This same energy is returned to me—I am met with kindness, compassion, understanding, acceptance, and love. I am drawn to individuals who can see, feel, and experience the Divine operating within me.*

I attract healthy and fulfilling relationships into my life. I am surrounded by individuals who exhibit the same Divine attributes as I. I am open and receptive to the unique gifts and blessings flowing to me through each individual with whom I remain in a relationship, and they are in turn blessed by my unique gifts that I pour forth in abundance. All of my relationships are beneficial to me and to my companions on the physical, emotional, and spiritual levels. I am surrounded by love and kindness; I am surrounded by caring, compassionate, and loving friends; I am never alone.

The treatment is spoken in the present tense, it is a declaration of the truth of me and of my experience, and it is phrased or spoken in such a way that the belief and conviction is held within it. I can say with complete honesty, all aspects of this treatment have come true in my experience, and I realize I must work to maintain the positive energy in myself in order to maintain these positive conditions that now exist in my life.

Step Five: THANKSGIVING

The next stage of a treatment is referred to as thanksgiving. In this stage of a treatment, we express gratitude for the knowledge that the gifts and blessings we set forth in the realization stage have come into our experience. We accept and own that the demonstration we desire has already occurred, and shifting into the energy of gratitude during prayer is an effective way to accomplish this. Similar to the other stages, it is critical to truly bring forth the energy and essence of pure gratitude and joy within you, for the realization that what you have prayed for has already come into your experience. Expressing gratitude and joy solidifies the belief or the faith that Divine Power and Intelligence is operating on your behalf to demonstrate your treatment.

> *I now give my thanks for the healing I know is occurring within me. I feel completely renewed and refreshed, as these worn-out and limiting beliefs are cast aside and taken away from my experience. I give thanks for my emotional and spiritual growth and development. I am now filled with joy and gratitude for the relationships I have. I am overjoyed by the blessings and gifts flowing between my companions and me. I express my gratitude for the memories, the experiences, the sharing, the connection, the support, the love, and the kindness coming into my experience and pouring forth from me into the lives of those with whom I am connected. I am grateful for an abundance of supportive, caring, loving, understanding, and compassionate individuals in my life.*

Step Six: RELEASE

The final stage of a treatment is referred to as release. I also like to refer to this stage as surrender. The energy and essence of pure surrender to close our spiritual mind treatments produces a powerful expression of deep faith, absolute trust, conviction, and unwavering belief. This energy places our trust fully in God, the Universe, Creative Intelligence. The act of surrendering creates the belief, it implies a trust, and it establishes a knowing and a deep conviction of a Power greater than ourself working and operating on our behalf to manifest perfect experiences in alignment with our intentions. This is the moment when we place our trust and belief in a higher power and open ourselves to receiving.

I now release and surrender these intentions into the perfect action of Divine Law. I place my trust fully that as I have spoken, as I believe, it is already done unto me. I recognize the Divine truth within me healing and dissolving any false beliefs limiting my experience. I recognize there is a Perfect Power already operating on my behalf, moving right now to align the circumstances, the people, and the events necessary to bring healthy relationships and lasting companions into my life experience. I let go, and I allow God to do Its work, and I accept my greatest good as it flows to me. And so it is.

Holmes provides us with the following advice: "Treat and move your feet." We must remember we are moving our feet to place ourselves in circumstances to promote and allow our good to come to us, holding our belief and our trust in Divine Law. For example, I cannot offer a treatment for new friendships and relationships and sit on the couch in my home and isolate myself, expecting new friends to show up and knock on my door. However, there is a balancing act between moving our feet versus crossing the threshold into the egoic realm of trying to force or control our circumstances. I believe a clear sign to know when that threshold is crossed is available in our emotional state. The instant we start to feel disappointment, frustration, or discouragement as we are moving our feet, this is a signal to us. It is a sign we have shifted from the energy of surrender, of trust, and of belief into the energy of forcing or controlling. Without remaining in the essence of true surrender, we diminish our belief, we diminish our trust, and we may sabotage our treatments.

The truth is, our little controlling self can never create or bring a manifestation into our experience nearly as beautiful, as perfect, and as miraculous as God can. God created this entire universe and keeps it all in perfect harmony at every single moment. It is so vast and beautiful, so awe-inspiring, we cannot even comprehend it with our sensory minds. So why not trust in this Power? If It can create the universe, your body, and keep all of creation operating and in existence in perfect peace and harmony, then It can certainly line up the circumstances, people, connections, and experiences necessary to manifest the intentions held within our treatments. Faith in this Perfect Power is the foundation for spiritual mind treatments and for conscious, effective prayers that result in tangible demonstrations. Holding belief and faith in this Power is what creates healing and allows miracles to unfold.

Because we are dealing with habitual thinking and emotional patterns that have been operating within us, possibly for decades, it may be unrealistic to expect a drastic and profound change overnight after one treatment. Our thoughts, beliefs, and emotions have a tendency to revert back to their old ways and keep us in a rut. Dr. Joe Dispenza goes into great detail about the neuroscience and biochemistry behind this in *Breaking the Habit of Being Yourself.* In essence, he explains that we become quite addicted to our habitual modes of thinking and being. Our bodies and cells are addicted to the chemical cocktails produced by our glands when we experience habitual emotional reactions. Further, our brains become hard wired to continue thinking in certain ways because deep and familiar pathways between neurons become well-established over time. Our bodies, our brains, and our minds have a strong tendency to resist change. Changing these beliefs and thought patterns that have been operating for decades can take a considerable amount of effort.

Ernest Holmes offers guidance in *The Science of Mind* to continue performing treatments until a clear and undeniable demonstration occurs. As he discusses in *How to Use the Science of Mind Principles in Practice,* if we are diligent and give fifteen to twenty minutes a day to our spiritual mind treatments, within one year we will be able to look back at ourselves and recognize profound shifts in our experiences. I will attest to this statement as a fact, and I continue to experience this year after year as I continue my healing work. I began more than seven years ago, and I now have no recognition of who I was or how I used to operate before I started these practices. I am a completely new person, and I have called in a completely new life in alignment with my values, my goals, and the positive energy I sustain.

I spent several years doing regular spiritual mind treatments similar to the one I shared above. I used these to attack and dissolve every limiting core belief I held within my subconscious mind related to my abuse. I did this work on an almost daily basis, alongside my meditation practice. In essence, I shined a light on my limiting beliefs through the meditation, then uprooted them and replaced them with far more beneficial and positive beliefs in alignment with the truth of who I am and with what I want in my life. I completely turned my life around and became an entirely new person through these practices.

The reality of this is that it takes time, effort, and continuous practice. However, you will start to see results, feel changes and shifts occurring within you, and start to see outward changes in your experiences shortly after setting the intention for healing and beginning this work. There is a response from the universe immediately in alignment with your intentions. Once you start seeing results, feeling those shifts within you, and watching demonstrations in your outward experience, you will find the motivation to continue and dive deeper.

Other Methods of Prayer

Spiritual mind treatment is also referred to as affirmative prayer by Centers for Spiritual Living. It is given this title because we are affirming or declaring the truth of ourselves. We are praying with positive words, positive intentions, and holding positive energy. Further, the act of praying in the present tense creates the conviction that our good is already here right now and available to us; we just need to open ourselves up with faith and accept it. However, we may find difficulty maintaining this energy or these intentions as we move through our busy, day-to-day lives. So, another effective form of prayer taught through Centers for Spiritual Living to help us maintain and sustain the energy of our treatments is referred to as affirmations.

In a class I took called "The Power of Your Word," I learned that we will not do ourselves much benefit if we take twenty minutes in the morning to conduct our spiritual mind treatments, then go through the remaining hours of our day stewing in negative thoughts about ourselves or our experiences. This reflects the difficulty in overcoming our thought and belief patterns because they have become habits. It requires a fairly constant practice of self-awareness and being present to catch ourselves when we drift into those habitual modes of thinking.

Affirmations are a useful tool to bring yourself back into the energy, the belief, and the conviction present when you stated your treatment. They are meant to be short, simple, one- or two-sentence declarations we can make to bring ourselves back to the truth we desire. Similar to our treatments, they must be declared in the present tense and with conviction to be effective. When we catch ourselves going into habitual modes of thinking, we can immediately say, "Aha!," and state an affirmation in alignment with the energy of the treatment we wish to demonstrate. Ideally, we can summarize the realization stage of our treatment with a few positive words and repeat these to ourselves throughout our days. The more often we do this, the more our thinking and beliefs start to shift and the greater our self-awareness becomes. We experience longer and longer durations of time when we are thinking (or praying) positively and consciously. The Law responds in kind.

In addition to the use of affirmations, I have found the use of Sanskrit mantras to be another beneficial and effective tool to create and sustain "right thinking" and the positive emotional states associated with my treatments. Mantra, directly translated, literally means mind control. Mantras have been used as a form of prayer in many Eastern religious traditions, particularly Hinduism and Buddhism.

In his book *Healing Mantras*, Thomas Ashley-Farrand discusses how the specific sounds and syllables used in Sanskrit carry tremendous power and intention behind them. He explains that the mantras included in his book were assembled to pray for specific intentions and have been used for these specific purposes for thousands of years. Ashley-Farrand presents mantras used for a variety of purposes: removing obstacles, finding forgiveness or compassion, cleansing an unwanted emotional state of being, calling in relationships, healing physical conditions, developing athletic strength, developing a deeper connection with Spirit, calling in material wealth. The list is endless.

Similar to affirmations, I used many of these mantras for specific purposes related to healing from the effects of my abuse. It can be difficult at times during meditation or while trying to work through a spiritual mind treatment to hold the positive thinking and emotion. Our minds and thoughts often want to wander. Although this is completely normal and natural and is not something to become upset over, I found it useful to have other tools available to me to bring my mind back to where I wished it to be. Using these mantras was effective for me. In addition to using spiritual mind treatments, I also used mantras during my regular prayer and meditation practice. Similar to affirmations, I used mantras throughout my day when I caught my thoughts or mind wandering into old and worn-out patterns that I wanted to change.

Using mantras was effective for me for two reasons. The first I discussed briefly in the previous chapter: The use of sound or vibration has the effect of helping me enter into deeper meditative states. Chanting these mantras repeatedly while working the beads of a mala gave my brain something to do besides think. As I chanted these sounds repeatedly, I found myself shifting into a theta brain wave state, in which thoughts are no longer occurring. The second reason: The act of focusing on and speaking a foreign language helped me achieve a stronger hold on the intention I was praying for. I found when I held an intention for healing a particular emotional condition and used a specific mantra presented in Ashley-Farrand's book, I had an easier time maintaining and strengthening the energy of the intention within my heart by chanting the sounds repeatedly.

Many of my limiting fears or false beliefs were revealed to me in meditations when I achieved inductions through chanting mantras. I recommend Ashley-Farrand's book to anyone who wishes to dedicate themselves to a regular prayer practice but struggles to keep their mind or heart focused on a specific intention.

Focus Your Prayers on Yourself Only

One important concept to keep in mind when we are doing our prayer work is that we are doing this work only on ourselves. There may be individuals in our lives who contribute to unwanted conditions, however, we cannot initiate or force change in them through prayer. We all have the gift of our own free will. People will not change unless they want to change. We have to change ourselves, and if individuals act or behave in undesirable ways, then we must take action and set healthy boundaries for ourselves.

There is folly in trying to change others by using prayer. Thomas Hora, in his book *One Mind,* describes this act as a trespass against another individual. We cannot pray to change others because it is an attempt to violate their free will. Trying to influence someone through prayer is an attempt to force, control, manipulate, or change an individual. The Law will not respond to us in this manner, because it cannot work against another's free will or against the intentions they hold for themselves.

Before I understood this concept, I prayed for close to two years for my second wife to change her behavior. Not surprisingly to me now, this had no effect on her or on our relationship. In fact, the dynamics present in our relationship worsened because I was not addressing my role in the situation. It is clear to me what I really needed to be praying for was myself, for my own healing, so I could wake up and realize who and what I truly was and own the fact that I need not maintain unhealthy relationships. I also needed to pray for the empowerment and confidence to assert myself, set my boundaries, and take action when they were not respected.

The only time we should ever pray for another individual is when we have permission to and when they clearly communicate their intention to us. Then we can understand what exactly it is they wish to change or achieve and can hold that intention for them in prayer support. When it comes to our healing work through prayer, our time and energy is most effectively spent working on ourselves and changing our own limiting thoughts and beliefs. The changes we desire in our experiences will then come about naturally, and we will be more clear to make conscious decisions about how to respond to undesirable conditions brought about by others.

CHAPTER • 9

Conscious Writing

I can attribute much of the development of my self-awareness, my emotional processing, and my healing to writing and journaling. The practice of writing immediately following a meditation exercise in particular has had a tremendous healing impact on me. If you truly want to feel an emotion and release it, then I would encourage you to write it out by hand with pen and paper. The act of writing out an emotion transfers the energy from within and releases it in the form of the ink on the pages. If there is any doubt about this energy transfer, one only needs to ponder why we experience sadness, joy, anger, or compassion when we read another individual's writing that expresses these emotions. That emotional energy was released from them, stored within the words written on the pages, and then flows through us as readers before being released. It is a transfer of energy, and it has the power to heal.

If you truly wish to embody and absorb the energy of a positive emotion such as love, kindness, compassion, or peace; write it out. Just as writing has the effect of releasing suppressed negative emotions, it also has the opposite effect of causing positive emotions and energy to grow and expand. If this seems difficult to accept, then I encourage you to spend one week writing about what kindness and compassion looks like in your life. Do this daily. Then observe your own actions and how you feel at the end of the week and see if you can discern an increased desire to be kind.

If you want to experience gratitude, write what you are grateful for. If you want to experience love, write about times in your life when you have felt unconditional love, or write about the positive attributes you appreciate in someone you love. Similarly, if you want to release anger and resentments, write what it is you are angry and resentful about and allow the emotions to flow out of you onto the paper. If you want to release sadness and grief, write about the experiences that brought these emotions to you in the first place.

Writing has the same effect on prayer. If you want to feel and embody the essence of a spiritual mind treatment, then I encourage you to write it out. Putting the treatment into writing has the effect of amplifying the intentions behind it and of bringing forth the emotions, the conviction, and the faith that helps create the belief. I feel a tremendous surge of energy when I write my treatments, and I maintain a consistent practice of written prayer work. When I go back and read my treatments, I reabsorb and expand the same energy I felt when I initially put my intentions in written form. An added benefit of written prayer work is the excitement and increased faith that comes when the treatment is demonstrated. I find it rewarding to write about how the treatment I released days or months ago was demonstrated in my experience, especially when there is a prior written record of the treatment. I believe the same will be true for you.

Oftentimes when I do prayer work for individuals who come to me for support, I write out my treatments for them. I have had countless individuals tell me that they print my treatments or keep them to read over and over again. What I know is happening in the process is that I am creating the needed emotion and conviction within me as I write out the treatment, and I am transferring that energy into the pen and onto the paper or into my fingers on the keys. The energy and conviction are then absorbed by the individuals who read my prayers, and they can embody the intentions I held for them. To me, it is a tangible transfer of energy and emotion, and I have personal experience that it works.

Journaling as a Spiritual Practice

I first began a spiritual writing practice shortly after I started attending my church. I attended a workshop offered by our Men's Ministry in which we were taught the practice of keeping a gratitude journal to maintain the energy of being grateful. When we experience and express gratitude on a regular basis, we draw more experiences to us allowing us to continue experiencing the same emotion. It also results in a shift in our awareness toward the things we have and our appreciation of them, rather than ruminating on things we do not have or circumstances we do not currently appreciate. I immediately saw the wisdom in this and began not only keeping a gratitude journal, but also using a journal to write down my prayers, my intentions, my visions, and my goals.

Using journaling as a means for emotional processing and developing self-awareness began shortly after I embarked on my healing journey. My journey started when I read Dr. Joe Dispenza's book *Breaking the Habit of Being Yourself* and doing the writing exercises he recommends. At the same time, I was taking the introductory course called "Beyond Limits," offered by Centers for Spiritual Living. Both of these avenues provided me with tools to help me to dig up and expose my own limiting core beliefs and to start seeing how they were playing out in my life.

As part of his recommendations for initiating healing and change, Dispenza asks his readers to write out every possible way a specific repetitive emotional reaction shows up in their experience: what thoughts precede the onset of the reaction, what the emotion feels like in their bodies when it is active, what thoughts occur while they are consumed by the emotion, and what actions they engage in while experiencing the emotion.

The activity of writing all of this out is a beneficial exercise in humility, and it also serves as an effective means to develop self-awareness. Dispenza offers guided meditation exercises to help individuals go within and visualize all of this after they write it out. He has his readers listen to the thoughts associated with a particular emotional reaction, focus on how it *feels* in their bodies, and watch themselves in their mind's eye as they engage in behaviors to deal with the emotion. He also asks his readers to visualize artificial circumstances that could cause the emotional reaction to arise. Then he has the individual shift the thoughts occurring in the moment and consciously choose a new way of being or a new response.

From personal experience, I can attest that doing this work is eye-opening. I found the more often I did this work, the more frequently I could feel and be completely aware of a particular emotional reaction arising in my body. It became easier to recognize how certain things felt in my body at the onset of a particular emotion. It then became easier to identify the thoughts occurring before the emotion arose and to listen to them as the emotion operated within me. Through time and practice, less effort was required to shift my thoughts, to choose a different response to the circumstance, and to act in a conscious manner with choice rather than going to an automatic, programmed reaction. This is what Eckhart Tolle refers to in *The Power of Now* as being the "silent watcher," and what Thomas Hora refers to in *One Mind* as being a "transcendent observer." It is the power of being fully present and fully self-aware in any given moment.

However, one key observation I made with continued practice of Dispenza's techniques was that they did not produce the desired effect I had in mind of altogether eliminating certain repetitive emotional reactions from arising within me. I had developed my self-awareness to recognize them, and I had learned a useful skill set to shift, redirect, and choose a new response. But I was still left with having to process the emotion after the fact. I wanted certain emotional reactions, such as defensiveness and resentment, to go away entirely, and this was not occurring with continued practices of Dizpenza's methods.

I later learned this was because of my experiences of child abuse. Dispenza's techniques certainly assist with developing self-awareness and making shifts in our day-to-day experiences. But for me, they did not necessarily shed light on the underlying root or cause of certain habitual emotional reactions and behavioral patterns, particularly those related to past trauma. Using his techniques did not help me bring my awareness to my suppressed emotions or my limiting core beliefs caused by my experiences of abuse. His book does not mention core beliefs and does not seem to address deeply suppressed emotions related to trauma or the ways in which these can play out in our life experiences. I had to go deeper with my work.

The techniques I developed for myself and my own healing are quite similar to what Dispenza teaches, but the difference is mine are aimed at actually uprooting the core beliefs and the suppressed emotions operating *behind* the habitual emotional reactions and behavioral patterns. Rather than attacking and changing a symptom (an outward reaction or behavior), my goal was to attack and dig up the entire root and cause behind my own patterns.

Writing Out Your Limiting Core Beliefs

What I encourage you to do as a spiritual practice related to the meditation exercises I recommend in Chapter Six is this: Once a core belief or repressed emotion is revealed to you in meditation, write it out. Next, read it aloud to yourself. If you are holding onto it, there will be strong emotion associated with it when you verbalize it. To assist you with processing repressed emotions and to enhance the exercises in visualizing past experiences when a particular emotion occurred, you will find that writing out all the memories you can recall when you experienced the emotion is also beneficial.

Once you write out a core belief and understand that you have adopted it, conscious writing around it and additional meditation work is necessary to fully understand how it has played out in your life and how it is still playing out. In developing my own self-awareness, I found it beneficial to write down the details I discovered related to my limiting core beliefs. Having gone through abuse, what I came to realize was there were several I had to dig up through time and then address. There were unique behaviors, emotional reactions, and repetitive circumstances showing up in my life related to each of these.

Once I had clarity around a particular core belief and the emotion(s) associated with it, I found that it became easy to discern all the ways in which those beliefs and emotions played out in my life. The most humbling part of this exercise was writing out how they currently operated in the present. I found looking at my addictive and compulsive behaviors especially difficult.

Similar to Dispenza's recommendations, the goal with my method is to write down as many memories and experiences as you can related to a particular core belief. It is important to also write down the emotional reactions associated with the beliefs. When working with present life experiences, I find it beneficial to pay attention to and write down how those particular emotions feel in my body when they arise, and I believe this will also be true for you. This exercise brings your recognition and awareness to how a particular core belief feels and the emotions associated with it. Write down the repetitive thoughts that come in when a particular belief or the emotions associated with it are triggered, so you develop familiarity with the unconscious thought patterns related to the belief.

Dream Journaling as a Spiritual Practice

Another beneficial conscious writing exercise I recommend is maintaining a dream journal while you do this work. I discovered my dreams and the repetitive themes within them were primarily products of memories, beliefs, and suppressed emotions buried in my subconscious. I found a dream journal to be an effective method to understand what was going on in my subconscious mind by recording and interpreting my dreams. Identifying recurring themes within my dreams led me to an awareness of a particular area I needed to heal.

Many realizations came to me by exploring my dreams. Repetitive dreams that persisted into adulthood of the girl I had a crush on in elementary school came to an end once I made the association of this dream to my fears of loneliness. Repetitive dreams about conflict with my mother led to the realization of the ongoing conflict and dynamics that existed between us. When I made these realizations and began establishing boundaries in this relationship, the dreams stopped.

Another realization I had through dreams involved my second wife, Anna. At the height of the stress and the abuse occurring in our relationship, I had an extremely vivid and realistic dream about her. We were driving in separate vehicles through steep terrain in a rainstorm. A mudslide came down into the road and impacted her car, which was in front of me. She lost control of her vehicle and veered through a guardrail, then careened over a cliff, plunging into a raging, muddy river below. At the last second, I deliberately made a choice to follow and swerved my truck off the road over the cliff edge. As it was free falling toward the river, I climbed out onto the hood and jumped to the riverbank. I wedged my feet into some exposed tree roots on the bank, then I plunged my upper body into the river and groped around for her and found her hand. I pulled her out of the car, out of the muddy river to safety on the bank. For the longest time, I interpreted this dream to mean I was somehow supposed to save her or fix her. I believed this was a sign that I was to remain in the relationship and wait for her to heal and support her toward her healing.

Soon after I divorced her, I attended a healing meditation service. I set an intention for my own healing around the pain and uncertainty I was going through around this divorce. Shortly after the meditation, the clarity around this dream showed up as I wrote out the details and contemplated the meaning. I realized the dream had nothing to do with saving or fixing her. Rather, it was meant to show me the level of risk I was willing to take on by trying to fix or change someone. I realized I was a "fixer," and I realized I was using this pattern as a means to distract myself from my own healing work. I realized I was willing to put myself into a potentially dangerous situation and completely compromise my boundaries to fix someone and to remain in a relationship with them. It was a powerful realization, and it resulted in a dramatic shift in how I show up in my current relationships.

In addition to writing down conscious memories and emotional conditions operating during your waking moments, writing out dreams and trying to understand recurring themes of emotional patterns during your sleeping moments is beneficial and can be quite revealing. I had many healing revelations come to me with this practice.

The Benefits of Writing as a Spiritual Practice

The benefit of all of this writing is twofold. First, when circumstances and experiences trigger those habitual beliefs (and they will), now you are developing awareness and familiarity around them. As the emotions rise in your body and the familiar feelings present themselves, it is easier to step aside as the silent watcher, and observe the condition and the familiar reaction. The same holds true for thought patterns.

It is from this space of self-awareness and discernment that spiritual mind treatment comes into play to continue healing the belief, changing the thought patterns, and shifting into a conscious response rather than a habitual, unconscious reaction. As experiences in my life triggered these reactions, I also found it beneficial to write about them and to write out the emotions, the thoughts, and the responses I had (even if I failed and fell back into an unconscious habitual reaction). In doing this, you begin to document and measure your progress toward healing these old wounds.

The second benefit of all of this writing is that it is both healing and liberating. I have come across many authors of New Thought literature who recommend similar writing exercises. In her book of soul exploration, *Entering the Castle,* Caroline Myss has her readers write out every detail that becomes apparent through meditation on how fear operates in in their lives. She also suggests writing about chaos, humiliation, and superstitious beliefs around God, just to name a few of her many introspective exercises.

In *The Spontaneous Fulfillment of Desire,* Deepak Chopra recommends writing exercises to help you discern your life's purpose or draw comparisons between yourself and others to help release judgment, to name a couple of examples.

In all of the classes I have taken to become a CSL-licensed practitioner, there is written homework around this same type of introspection and development of self-awareness around our emotions and thought patterns. It is clear this type of conscious writing has a well-recognized beneficial healing effect.

What I realized through all of this writing—completed while being completely honest with myself about thought patterns I had, emotional reactions that showed up, and behaviors I exhibited to deal with certain emotions—was this: It was reminiscent of confession from back when I was involved in the Catholic Church. I used to scoff at this practice, mainly because I felt it had largely lost its purpose. Going in and sitting down with a priest and rattling off random sins—"I stole a candy bar from a store," "I cursed at someone," "I fought with my spouse"—and then being told to repeat ten Hail Mary's and ten Our Father prayers had little benefit or healing power for me. By comparison, actually sitting and consciously writing out all the ways these limiting core beliefs and repressed emotions showed up and played out in my life, and actually admitting to it and owning it, was indeed humbling.

Essentially, this all boils down to writing out a thorough confession and bringing your awareness to these behaviors, positioning them front and center. There is no denial. You are being completely honest and authentic with yourself and essentially exposing your little self to your higher self. I believe this is supposed to be the original intent behind the Catholic sacrament of confession, but in my experience, the intention and the power behind it were not there. The other aspect of confession that was supposed to be beneficial was doing this work with a priest, who ideally would have maintained the energy of compassion, understanding, and healing. It is indeed liberating (and necessary) to share these insights and this work with compassionate individuals who will hold you in healing and prayer consciousness, which I will address in the next chapter.

This practice of conscious writing is humbling. Owning who you are and how you show up in life in ways you may not be proud of is a profound expression of humility. Experiencing humility, then having compassion and understanding for yourself around how these behaviors and habits came into being and why they continue to play out, moves you into a state of self-compassion and self-forgiveness. Once you do this work on yourself, you then can shift your awareness to why others in your life, particularly abusers, acted in the ways they did. Having compassion and forgiveness toward yourself increases your ability to show compassion and move into forgiveness for them.

Writing Out New and Beneficial Beliefs

As a final recommendation for your writing practice, similar to writing out the limiting beliefs you wish to heal, I encourage you to write out the new beliefs you wish to adopt to replace them. Write out the ways in which you see yourself showing up related to these new beliefs. Write out the thought patterns you will have around your new and beneficial beliefs. Write out how you will feel and what it looks like when you begin to exhibit these new beliefs, thought patterns, and emotions in your daily life. Write out how these new emotions feel in your body. Write out your spiritual mind treatments related to your healing and related to embodying these new beliefs.

From this writing work, move into meditation and use the same visualizing process discussed in Chapter Six to see yourself living with this new energy. Feel the energy of your treatments, feel the emotions arising within you when you speak the treatments, and feel the emotions arise within you as you visualize yourself behaving in ways associated with these new beliefs.

Through time, through continued awareness and by making the shifts away from the old patterns, through continued meditation, through spiritual mind treatments, and through journaling, you will find you no longer have any familiarity with these old worn-out beliefs. You will also be able to see how the new beliefs you planted into your subconscious are playing out in new and beneficial ways. You will become a completely new and changed individual and will no longer have any recognition of who you were in your past or how you operated. Your recognition of your progress will continue to unfold as you continue with this work.

I have heard many individuals lament that they are not good writers, so therefore they do not keep journals. Do not allow your ego to sabotage your efforts in this way. When it comes to your healing work, conscious writing is conscious writing, and it cannot be good or bad. The intention is to heal. Regardless of the form your writing takes, if you use it to release suppressed painful emotions and embody positive energy, then your purpose is accomplished. The goal is not to produce a best-seller or a candidate for a Pulitzer Prize. The goal is to release suppressed emotions and beliefs, develop self-awareness, and embody new beneficial beliefs about yourself. Write in a style and a manner that works for you. No one is going to read this material other than you.

CHAPTER • 10

Conscious Relationships

All of the inner work and emotional processing we explored to this point can be intense and painful. We bring up memories of traumatic experiences, painful emotions, and beliefs that have been suppressed for years, possibly even decades. It is important and beneficial to have a loving and supportive network of friends, mentors, perhaps a loving partner, and possibly a therapist or other practitioner to support us as we engage in this work.

While I did most of this work on my own in the privacy of my home, I spent just as much time sharing my experiences, realizations, memories, and the emotions I felt or processed with very close and trusted friends. Talking through these things with authenticity in the company of individuals who know how to listen with compassion and empathy is yet another avenue to facilitate healing. Just as writing it out in a journal helps you release the emotions, talking it out with a trusted friend (or many friends), mentors, a partner, a therapist, or a practitioner also creates a space where you can release painful emotions.

A professional may be needed to process the more difficult aspects of buried pain. However, I encourage you to establish conscious relationships with emotionally healthy and trustworthy individuals and to share your experiences with them. I found that the relationships that blossomed through sharing my experiences with individuals on the same path as I to be far more rewarding and life-giving than what I experienced in a professional setting working with a therapist.

There is great value in sharing your experiences, not only for yourself but also for those with whom you maintain healthy relationships. I will go as far to say this is something we each need and crave in our life, and for good reason. We are not meant to be islands, and we are not meant to be in solitude. We are social beings. We are meant to connect with, heal with, grow with, learn from, and teach by sharing with others and listening to them.

As we are doing this work and waking up, as we develop our self-awareness, and as we learn what boundaries we want to maintain for our own self-care and self-love, something else beneficial starts to happen. If doing this work brings you to your first true awakening, as it did for me, you will likely find that a dramatic shift in your relationships soon follows. Individuals who are emotionally asleep tend to engage or remain in relationships with others who are similarly asleep. You may find many of your relationships no longer fit or are not in alignment with the new experiences you wish to manifest. Or you may find those you are in relationships with do not understand when you try to express what you are going through.

For those of us who have experienced prolonged abuse in our lives, a truth we have to come to grips with is that we often show up in our relationships in dysfunctional ways until we wake up. More than likely, we have attracted other individuals into our experience who exhibit similar dysfunction in their behaviors when relating on deeper and more intimate levels. The energy we release attracts more of the same right back to us, as like attracts like. The other truth is that we may not know this or have awareness of it until we experience healthy and conscious relating with someone else who is awake. Our lack of awareness is a function of never having experienced something different, more beneficial, healthier, or uplifting. For many of us, all we have ever known or lived with are dysfunctional relationships. They become familiar and comfortable to us.

This brings up a word of caution regarding who you choose to share your experiences with. You may experience shocking realizations, achieve personal growth, relive painful memories, and perhaps encounter deep, profound spiritual experiences and dramatic healing moments while doing this work. You will become far more aware of your not-so-pleasant habits and behavioral patterns and where they stem from. You must use discernment and clarity in choosing who you relate with and who you share these experiences with. As is written in the New Testament, "Do not give what is holy to the dogs, and do not throw your pearls before swine, or they will trample them under their feet, and turn and tear you to pieces" (Matthew 7:6, The New King James Version). It is most beneficial to share with individuals who know how to listen to you, who can be present when they listen, who maintain conscious energy of compassion toward you, who affirm you, who support you, and who build you up. This growth, the healing that comes with it, and the spiritual experiences that show up are your pearls of great value. Share them wisely and only with those whom you can trust.

I learned this lesson the hard way. When I first began my process of awakening, I was still married to Anna, and I tried to maintain the relationship for an additional year. It seems natural to have a desire to share these experiences with a spouse. However, the reality of this marriage was she regularly resorted to emotional abuse during most of our disagreements and conflicts. All of these intimate and vulnerable details I shared so openly with her she ultimately used as weapons to intentionally trigger pain, shame, or guilt during disagreements. This constituted the most difficult form of emotional abuse I have ever experienced in my life, and I felt completely betrayed. Through these extremely hurtful experiences I learned this crucial lesson around using my own discernment.

My Support Network of Male Mentors

The first time I experienced healthy relating—in which openness and authenticity were front and center, in which there was no judgment or criticism, in which no one was trying to fix me or give me unwanted advice, and in which there was active and present listening with compassion—was with other men. I have moved completely through my forgiveness work for my parents, particularly my father. An important piece of that was learning to accept my father exactly how he was and where he was in his life experience without trying to change him. I knew I would not be able to have a deep, intimate, vulnerable, or authentic relationship with him. At the same time, I knew I needed men in my life, particularly older men with wisdom and experience, to fill that role. I wanted mentors. I wanted older men who had been through the same trenches I had been in and who healed themselves. I wanted their guidance. I wanted older men who could teach me by example and from their experiences to do things differently than what I learned growing up. I wanted father figures. I wanted to learn to be a true gentle man.

I set these intentions when I was in my twenties, long before I learned about Science of Mind or understood the principles behind maintaining faith. I realize now that when I set these intentions, I knew and had faith God would provide me with exactly what I needed. I have been blessed, as seven father figures have come into my life since I set these intentions. These men are all highly spiritual. They carry tremendous wisdom; they admire and love me; and they all provide me with the guidance and level of intimacy I craved from older, father-like figures. The best part of this demonstration is the perfection of these men to fit specific roles I needed and some of the serendipitous commonalities I had with each of them. I maintain close relationships with all of them to this day.

The first of these men showed up at a time when I was spiraling out of control at the tail end of my marriage to Rebecca. During this time, my relationship with her was practically nonexistent. There was little romantic attraction or intimacy between us. My older son, Dillon, was a toddler at this time, and disagreements over how to maintain expectations and boundaries for him were driving Rebecca and me further apart. I was traveling quite a bit for work and was operating at the peak of my compulsive behaviors around sex, women, and masturbation, as I described previously.

Rebecca had just been diagnosed with a relapse of depression and an anxiety disorder, which I suspected had been going on for many months prior.

I was a mess and at a complete loss for what to do. I realized I was spinning out of control with my behaviors when I worked out of town. I realized I was no longer attracted to Rebecca, and I had serious doubts of being able to rebuild our connection. I reached out to a church I attended at the time that offered spiritual counselors who volunteered to help people in crisis. This is how I met the first true father figure in my life, who was in his sixties at the time.

He was the first individual with whom I shared my struggles and shortcomings who just listened. He did not judge me, did not condemn me, and did not offer me unwanted advice. He kept affirming that I was a good person doing my best and that God and others loved me. He gave me books to read, which was my first exposure to New Thought principles. Over time, I developed enough trust with him that I began asking him for advice, and he helped me navigate through my first divorce, the affair I was involved in, and my second divorce. He had a kind way of bringing me to the realization that chasing after women constantly was not going to serve me. Rather than criticizing me, he was always compassionate and supportive. I have no idea where I would be or what further messes I would have brought into my experience had I not met him at that time.

As it turned out, he was also emotionally abused as a child, primarily by his father. He also went through a difficult divorce with children involved, and he helped raise them as a single father. One of the most significant commonalities we had is we both operated as "fixers." He had a pattern in his earlier life of getting involved with women who were not emotionally healthy or available, and he would try to fix them or change them. Listening to his stories helped me see this in myself. He helped me see that this was a means of distracting from working on or fixing myself. He also helped me see that as a fixer, all I was doing was attracting "broken" individuals into my experience. It was beneficial and serendipitous to meet someone who exhibited the same patterns in their relationships I was engaging in. It was also healing to discuss these habits with someone who had already worked through them and could give me advice and support with compassion and wisdom from life experience, while not being judgmental.

    The second of these men who came into my experience was also harshly abused by his father, and he shared an impactful story with me around the forgiveness work he accomplished toward his father. I met him through my job, and we seemed to establish an immediate connection around spirituality, introspection, and shared experiences related to past traumas. Like me, he struggled with addictive behaviors to avoid dealing with his pain. Also similar to me, he had a habit when he was younger of chasing after women and jumping from one relationship to another as a coping mechanism. Listening to his stories helped me admit to my own addictive compulsions and helped me to start seeing how they were affecting my life. My conversations with him helped me realize how these compulsions controlled me and resulted in me engaging in relationships that were harmful to me on many levels. He was also never judgmental or critical in any of our intimate discussions, and he had a way of offering advice in a kind way, allowing me to do my growth and healing at my own pace.

The Men's Ministry at my current church connected me with five other older gentlemen who greatly assisted me in my healing journey, my self-realization, and my emotional processing. Joining this group was my first experience with such a deep level of intimacy, authenticity, openness, and vulnerability in a group setting. It was also the first time I experienced such openness among men within a group setting. Sharing my stories and my emotional processing with these men greatly facilitated my healing. I also discovered specific commonalities with each of them.

One of them also went through a high-conflict divorce, and he helped me navigate my second divorce. He was what CSL refers to as a prayer practitioner at the time, and he regularly provided me with prayer support and a listening ear. He helped set me on the path of my own regular meditation practice by explaining the many benefits it had in his life. Most importantly, by example he taught me to send out my intentions for the right partner or companion and to just surrender and allow her to show up through my faith and belief, rather than trying to force it to happen.

Another of these men was abused by both of his parents. Similar to my own experiences, he struggled with addictive behaviors around his own sexuality. One of the best pieces of advice he gave me, which seems so obvious to me now, was "You don't have to try to marry every woman you end up dating." I experienced profound healing around my sexual issues in sharing with this man. At the time of our interactions, I was still carrying around a tremendous amount of guilt, shame, and self-disgust over my sexual habits and behaviors. I met this man during the final year of his life, and most of our interactions occurred while he was in hospice care just a month prior to his passing. He knew he was going to pass soon, and yet he still offered his time to allow me to visit and speak with him, for which I was and remain deeply grateful. Our mutual sharing helped me completely release all the negative energy I was holding onto related to my sexuality. My experiences with him remain a powerful and profound influence in my life. The most inspiring lesson I took from him was this: Even in a state of pain, suffering, and with death looming, he still gave of himself and of his time with compassion to help and support someone who was in need. I am forever grateful for my experiences with him on my life path.

I have a scientific and analytical mind, and I am highly organized. These traits greatly assist me in my engineering profession. However, these same traits can be a curse if I try to apply them in relationships, where feeling and empathy are more appropriate ways to support someone. Another of the men in our Men's Ministry spoke openly about having similar characteristics himself and how he used these characteristics inappropriately in relationships. He further shared the lessons he learned from the resulting consequences. Through him, I learned I cannot think or analyze my way through my emotions, nor should I ever attempt to do so when others are sharing their emotions with me.

He and I also learned we are both vivid dreamers, and we somehow had identical recurring themes run through our dreams over time. We have a deep connection over sharing our personal growth and our dream interpretations, and he is another person who listens and offers compassionate wisdom and guidance. He is one of the most supportive and affirming individuals I have ever met. He clearly sees my potential, understands my visions and goals, and continuously offers me praise and recognition as I continue on my life path and healing journey.

A commonality I share with another of these individuals is that we both identify as the so-called black sheep in our families, primarily because of our spiritual beliefs and practices. Like me, he grew up in a family who practiced and maintained a deep conviction in Roman Catholicism. Unlike me, while being taught at a young age to behave along a certain moral code through tactics that elicited guilt and shame in the congregation, he concluded and openly declared, "Well, this is all just complete bullshit." I unfortunately did not conclude until much later in life that this type of traditional Catholic teaching did not feel like the truth to me. He and I also share this same sentiment around the belief that Catholicism or any religious dogma and liturgical practices are the one and only true path to God or heaven or salvation.

His choice to seek other avenues for spirituality and his adoption of beliefs that are not in alignment with Catholic dogma resulted in an estrangement from some members of his family. I began to experience similar issues related to my own spiritual pursuits and beliefs, and he was able to provide me with guidance to navigate these challenges.

This individual in our Men's Ministry who went through the exact same experiences as I did helped me tremendously, as he helped me learn to process the emotions associated with the rejection and judgment my parents sent in my direction over my choices in my own spiritual journey. He made it simple for me to understand. He told me he primarily practiced

Buddhist teachings despite his Catholic upbringing. As he worded it, "My parents just don't like me very much, and I don't like them very much either. So we have all just decided to go our separate ways." Essentially, what he explained was his parents were intolerant of his beliefs and practices, and their constant criticism and judgment of him violated his boundaries and hurt him. He made the decision to accept this, maintain a healthy boundary for himself, and let them decide what kind of relationship they wanted with him.

I came to the same conclusion with my own parents. In a nutshell, I decided intolerance, and the judgment and criticism that comes with it, will not be tolerated. I openly and clearly communicated with my parents that a relationship cannot be possible unless they accept this boundary and cease their criticism and judgment of my church, my faith, and my spiritual practices. I became much more comfortable setting this boundary after sharing these common experiences with this man. It took my parents time, but they have eventually learned to respect this boundary of mine, and our relationship has been able to continue, with all of us having an agreement to be open and understanding of one another's spiritual preferences.

The last of these men, the seventh father figure in my life, shares many of the same spiritual gifts that I possess. I discuss throughout this book several dreams I have had that later came true. There is also a theme of deceased relatives showing up in my dreams, relatives who point out areas in my life or in my relationships that need to be healed. I also experience frequent dreams in which I can actually feel the emotional conditions and understand the mindset of individuals with whom I maintain close relationships or for whom I am asked to offer prayer support for any reason. I have learned that these are common characteristics of highly sensitive individuals and empaths. This last individual I wish to share about is a gifted empath, and he and I have developed a close relationship through sharing our experiences.

When I shared some of my dream experiences in our men's group, either the experience of my dreams coming true or of picking up the emotions of others, one man invited me to stick around afterward if I wanted to talk more about this.

He has proven to be a valuable mentor to help me understand what to do with these experiences. He has taught me how to process the emotions that come through these dreams, and he has provided me with assistance in interpreting my dreams. He has given me a tremendous amount of advice on how to use my discernment to decide if it is appropriate to share the content of these particular dreams with the individuals involved. He also has taught me techniques to release emotions or even physical symptoms that show up in my experience that may not belong to me, which is a common trait of empaths.

He opened me up to an entirely new world in which these gifts can be used to facilitate the healing of others who are receptive. This individual from our Men's Ministry taught me that the most useful characteristic empaths possess is that we are sensitive to and can feel the emotional conditions within another person. He has shared and I have since experienced that this is true, even if the individual has not actually brought their own awareness to the repressed emotions operating behind their outward conditions. In essence, if we can feel their emotions, then we can help to bring their awareness to their repressed emotions, which can facilitate their healing. I owe much of the knowledge I have gained around this phenomenon to this man, and I intend to use this gift as a prayer practitioner to help people who come to me for support in the future.

Each of these beneficial and life-giving relationships required work and effort on my part. Many more healthy relationships, ones I find beneficial on the spiritual and emotional levels, have come into my experience because of the skills I learned from these men.

I also maintain close, intimate, platonic relationships with women. Many of these women are such close friends, I feel as though they are my sisters, and the older ones serve as mother figures in my life. The primary work I had to do and the efforts I had to bring for these relationships to manifest and continue growing was the work of truly being myself. Most important, this required me to start truly loving and fully accepting myself.

Authenticity in Our Relationships

To cultivate these healthy and fulfilling relationships in my life, I had to learn to truly be myself. What I mean by being myself is being authentic, open, completely honest, direct, intimate, and vulnerable. In my past, because of my fears of loneliness, I spent my energy trying to get people to like me. This most often required me to put on a mask. It required me to show up in a way I thought or believed would be embraced by those I wanted as friends or by those I wanted as romantic partners. It often required me to sacrifice my boundaries, or to just not even define boundaries for myself, and to accept whatever treatment came my way. It was easier to engage and remain in unhealthy relationships than to communicate my preferences and boundaries, risk a conflict, and end up alone. My fears of loneliness and isolation resulted in unnecessary and unhealthy compromising around what I wanted from my relationships. The other aspect of this—constantly putting on a mask and, at times, wearing a different mask around different circles of people—drained the energy and life from me.

Truly healthy and conscious relationships are those in which you can show up as your authentic self, knowing you will be accepted and loved completely. A good sign for me to determine whether or not I was doing this was whether I felt drained or energized following my interactions.

Conversely, this type of conscious relationship required me to encourage those I engaged with to be their true and authentic selves, and for me to embrace them, love them, and accept them completely as they were. It took me a long time to figure out that accepting and loving someone completely does not equate to putting up with abusive behavior or compromising my boundaries, my self-love, or my self-care. Through time, I learned that truly loving myself and others must involve clear communication of boundaries and preferences. Sometimes this may involve a tougher form of love—withdrawing from a relationship when toxic behaviors persist.

Showing up as my true and authentic self equates to sharing openly with others, while using discernment to know whether or not it is safe. Through experience, I have learned how to determine who is safe and who is not. If I am met with a response of openness, understanding, and mutual sharing, I feel safe to open up to the individual. If I am met with criticism, judgment, silence, or a response unrelated to what I shared,

I take it as a sign the person is not someone I wish to relate with on a deep level.

For me, being authentic involves sharing my past and current experiences with humility, completely owning my part and the lessons I learned or am learning. It means being completely open and honest about the emotions that come from these experiences. It means admitting when I have been triggered by some circumstance or interaction and owning the reasons for it. It involves my willingness to allow my emotions to flow and be expressed if they are still raw and operating within me. To me, this defines true authenticity and vulnerability. It is exposing to others those raw and sore areas that may not be fully healed.

Showing up with authenticity, for me, also means getting crystal clear about the visions and goals I am pursuing in my life and sharing these with others. It means getting clear about my values and ethics, those I create for myself rather than those others project onto me. It involves making continuous and determined efforts to show up in alignment with those values and ethics. It also involves recognizing and affirming the visions and dreams others are pursuing and being respectful of their values and ethics, even if they are different from my own.

Non-Conditional Relating

Another practice I find to be beneficial in creating conscious relationships is non-conditional relating—in other words, letting go of expectations of getting, releasing attachments to wanting, and growing beyond the worn-out paradigm of, "If you scratch my back, then I will scratch yours." In my experience, creating conscious relationships required me to move beyond thinking patterns of "what can I get" to "what can I give unconditionally?" It is bestowing random acts of kindness for the sake of being kind to someone, rather than doing it in the hopes of getting something in return. It is showing up as a loving, compassionate, and caring individual toward someone else for the simple purpose of being a beneficial presence in their life and to nurture the relationship. In non-conditional relationships, there is also no desire or effort made to change, fix, or control anyone.

Non-conditional relating should not be confused with or equated to giving and sacrificing your time and energy at the expense of your own self-love and self-care. It should not be equated with continuously putting time and energy into a one-sided relationship in which you are being taken advantage of. Nor should it be equated with enabling someone who is seeking assistance while not owning responsibility for the problems they have created in their own life. Consider these examples. Is it beneficial and healthy to sacrifice your needed sleep to answer recurring late-night phone calls from the friend who is overanxious and continues to bring drama into their circumstances, who needs you to help make them feel better? If you are the only one reaching out, making attempts at connection and quality time, and interactions are only scheduled in consideration of the other party's preferences, is this mutually beneficial? Is taking an alcoholic relative into your home because they lost their job and have been evicted going to truly benefit them if they are not willing to engage in their own healing work?

I am not advocating for relationships without any expectations. This is not realistic. There is a big difference between setting expectations for getting or wanting things from others to make us feel good versus expectations in alignment with our self-love and self-care and realizing we alone are responsible for our own happiness. Each of us must use our individual discernment to understand the balancing act required in this dance occurring in our relationships. The truth is, if you define your boundaries and communicate them, then you have set your expectations.

I certainly set expectations and maintain them in my relationships. I expect my relationships to be mutually healthy and beneficial. I expect both parties to be completely open and honest and to communicate our boundaries and preferences. I also expect both parties to respect boundaries and preferences with one another. Lastly, I only engage in relationships in which the other person and I show up and accept each other as our authentic selves—no masks, no faking, no hiding, and no dishonesty.

I have found it rewarding to relate to individuals who share my same level of awareness and consciousness. I also have found that putting my energy and efforts into non-conditional relating with authentic and emotionally healthy individuals is far more beneficial than my old patterns, in which manipulation, control, desires to fix or change others, and power plays from both parties to get what they wanted were the normal dynamics.

Showing up authentically, being completely open and honest, and sharing vulnerabilities—this not only heals you, but it also facilitates healing in those around you. We are all one, and we all share common experiences. Every person you share your true self with will benefit, even if they do not outwardly express it or seem receptive toward you. Set the intentions and begin taking the steps to develop conscious relationships that will support you on your healing journey.

CHAPTER • 11

Conscious Service

Many people who experienced prolonged abuse as children tend to develop core beliefs of unworthiness, uselessness, and stupidity. We have thoughts that tell us we are a failure, and we have little to contribute. Nothing can be further from the truth.

These types of beliefs and thoughts completely handicap us. They limit our experience, and they restrict the flow of the Divine Power within us from being brought forth and expressed. This is one of the many unfortunate consequences and long-term effects of child abuse. As long as we carry these ideas and buy into them, we put our life and our purpose on hold. The reality is we each have unique gifts we are meant to identify, embrace, expand, and express into the world as beneficial presences. We are here to shine our lights. We are here to soar. We are here to thrive. And we are here to contribute in a beneficial manner.

What is the truth of these limiting beliefs we have adopted? The truth is that they do not belong to us; they are not ours. These beliefs and emotions were projected onto us by our abusers because this is what they believed about themselves, and this is how they felt in their own lives. It is painful to believe these things, and it is extremely unpleasant to go through the experiences we have as a result of carrying these emotions within us. Abusers do not know how to deal with their pain, and they do not know how to identify with or feel their emotions. As a result, one of the coping mechanisms they use, consciously or not, is projecting their own pain, their own emotions, and their own limiting beliefs onto others.

I am quite certain many of you who have gone through prolonged abuse in your lives can relate to having similar voices coming up in your minds:

> *I will never amount to anything. Why bother attempting this new task; I will probably fail. There is no way I can do this; I just don't know how. I do not want to get involved with this; I have nothing useful to contribute. I am not smart enough to take something like this on. Why should I go to this event? No one is going to like me or talk to me. I can't seem to do anything right. I am just not good at anything. I can't seem to finish any goals I set for myself. I will never be able to finish this in time.*

These are the types of thoughts stemming from limiting core beliefs and repressed emotions centered around unworthiness. What I am going to say about this type of thinking is this: It is all absolute bullshit. These are lies and false ideas projected onto us by others, or they have been adopted by our egos in response to how we were mistreated by others. There is no truth to any thoughts of this nature. These false ideas and beliefs are completely out of alignment and contradictory to who and what we truly are. They have no place within us; they are not compatible with our true energy; and they cannot coexist with our higher selves once we awaken.

So what is the truth of us, and what are some affirmations that resonate with our higher selves?

I am a light and an inspiration in the world. I succeed at every task I set my intentions on, and I put forth my best efforts. I learn the skills and acquire the resources to accomplish any goal I set for myself. I have unique gifts to contribute. Divine intelligence and wisdom operate within me at all times, and solutions to any obstacle are provided to me. I am a beneficial presence and a light to others, and I draw in healthy relationships. I do my best, and my best is enough. I learn from my mistakes and continually improve myself. I have incredible and unique skills, and I am attracted to opportunities in which they are put to good use. I work efficiently and effectively to accomplish my goals.

How does the energy of these statements feel within you compared to the negative ones written above? Which statements feel like the truth? As I mention in the Introduction to this book, positive thinking alone will not get us very far and will not result in tangible changes to our experience or any significant healing. First, the limiting beliefs and repressed emotions must be dug up, fully felt, and released. Then, new beliefs must be installed through spiritual mind treatments or other methods.

As my own healing progressed, I discovered that identifying my own gifts and ways I could use them through conscious service greatly reinforced new beliefs that I mattered, I had something to contribute, and I could be of beneficial service to others. Then, affirmations similar to what I have written here actually started to feel true for me and began demonstrating in my experience. The question is, how exactly do we go from feeling unworthy or that we have little to contribute to identifying our gifts and finding ways to express them?

In my experience, the gifts just showed up on their own through doing my healing work. I believe the gifts are already there, and there is no forceful process required to discover them, but we must do our healing work first. What I experienced, as I removed and let go of emotional baggage that had been repressed for decades, I created space and cleared restrictions for these gifts to start flowing. Then opportunities for me to express these gifts began coming into my experience on their own. All that was required of me was to set a conscious intention for my gifts to be revealed to me and for me to remain open and receptive as opportunities to express these gifts came into my experience. I also had to maintain a willingness to say yes.

A unique realization came to me through this process of discovering my gifts. I realized repressing my emotions created a significant block in allowing Spirit to communicate to me, flow through me, or express Itself through me as my gifts. I learned that if we repress our emotions, we are not allowing ourselves to feel. I believe Spirit communicates to us primarily through feelings and emotions, so if we do not allow ourselves to feel our emotions or our pain, then we certainly cannot feel Spirit communicating to us. Essentially, we repress the precise feelings Spirit uses to communicate with or to us: our intuition, our discernment, recognition of synchronicity in our experiences, seeing with spiritual eyes, or hearing with spiritual ears.

There is a unique feeling within that many of us are familiar with and identify as Spirit communicates to us. I imagine it is unique from person to person. For me, I become overwhelmed with energy coursing through my body. Physically, I get goosebumps all over my skin, though I am not cold. I refer to this sensation as "God bumps." I also feel a strong warmth, at times like fire, coming straight from my heart. This occurs when I receive an intuitive hit or when I meditate and ask for guidance around a decision and I allow my discernment instead of my ego to direct me. It occurs when I become fully present and feel peace within me, or as I soak in any aspect of nature and see that same energy moving through all of creation. I feel it when I have a profound realization that results in an emotional healing or release within me. It also comes when I see or hear the truth of some experience or circumstance. In other words, it happens when I understand and know the spiritual or emotional truth operating behind an outward condition.

This fire and warmth that came from my heart was strongest as I discovered ways I could bring my gifts forth in the world. It was strongest when I identified and began moving forward with what I believed to be my purpose in life. It is now most powerful when I fully envision my dreams and goals for using my gifts to their full potential in alignment with being a beneficial presence in the world. It is an overwhelming feeling of joy coming from within me, and I can best describe it as a surge of energy washing through my entire body. I feel it continuously vibrating in the background of my being as I take steps and move forward with intention toward my vision. I can also feel it when I take any action in my circumstances that allows me to bring my gifts into the world.

Using Our Gifts for Conscious Service

I believe these feelings are the most clear sign you can receive as far as what your gifts are or how you are supposed to use them. Then any type of decisive action you take when you use your gifts to make a beneficial contribution to others is what I define as conscious service. Engaging in conscious service is extremely rewarding. It not only serves as icing on the cake once you have progressed deeply into your healing work, it also serves as a beneficial spiritual practice to continue facilitating your healing journey.

I am not imposing any limitations or expectations by using the word service. This word can be interpreted as volunteer work, or giving our time and energy toward a cause outside of ourselves. Conscious service certainly does not have to be on a volunteer basis. Your entire career and vocation can be an expression of conscious service. Conversely, engaging in conscious service can be as simple as performing any activity in which your gifts are applied in a beneficial manner toward a definite purpose.

Conscious service should certainly not involve self-sacrifice or extreme compromise to our other commitments and responsibilities. Rather, it is an activity that brings us only joy. Calling it service also does not imply that we must forfeit the desire to be financially rewarded for our efforts. If you have a desire to become wealthy through conscious service, then find the means to compensate yourself in doing so. There is no better career to have than one in which you make money doing what you love the most.

As I define it, any activity we choose to engage in that allows us to use our gifts or the attributes we possess in alignment with the Divine Power existing within each of us qualifies as conscious service. Any activity we engage in while holding the intention to benefit and contribute to others in the world or in our direct experience also qualifies. It can be as simple as performing random acts of kindness. Or it can be as complex as taking in more than 25,000 abandoned children, taking care of them, rehabilitating them, and reintroducing them into society as empowered individuals, as Charles Mulli accomplished in Kenya.

Engaging in conscious service brings joy to others and improves their conditions. It also empowers us and contributes to our own growth and evolution. The way conscious service shows up in each of our lives is going to be unique, given our life circumstances, commitments, time, energy, passions, and, of course, the unique gifts we each possess.

I believe all of us have a degree of familiarity with at least some of our gifts, the unique abilities we possess that allow us to do things in life to bring us joy and to do them exceptionally well. It also seems we possess other gifts we may not even be aware of, gifts that seem to just show up unexpectedly as we progress through our healing work. As speaker and writer Tama Kieves says, "Our greatest challenges in life can become our greatest gifts."

I was in the early stages of my healing work when I heard Kieves make this statement, and now that I have progressed as far as I have, I fully understand what she means. Healing from the greatest challenges in my life—the trauma of abuse and neglect throughout my childhood and an abusive second marriage—absolutely became the greatest gifts I ever experienced. I have had so many blessings and such profound positive change in my experience because of my healing work. Many lessons and growth opportunities came from all of these experiences. I also have become aware of some unique abilities I possess, which were revealed to me as I progressed deeper.

Expressing Our Gifts through Authentic Sharing

One of the ways I chose to bring my own gifts into the world was to share my experiences, the realizations I have had, the lessons I learned, and the growth I went through with others. This is one of the simplest forms of conscious service we can engage in: sharing our healing journey with those who are receptive. This has a twofold beneficial effect. First, because of our connection with all of humanity, because we are truly one, we can remain certain that something we say or share with another individual will have a positive effect on them. At every workshop or spiritual group I ever attended where people shared with authenticity, I found something in their experience or story I could relate to and apply to my own experiences. We have the same effect on others through our own sharing. The other benefit of sharing in this manner is it accelerates your own healing process.

Sharing my experiences within my relationships—in my classes, in spiritual groups, and in workshops—became a powerful way for me to engage in conscious service. All that was required of me was to be real, to be completely open and vulnerable, and to be authentic. In doing this, I experienced the same response from countless individuals in a variety of settings: gratitude. At every practitioner class I attended through Centers for Spiritual Living, every workshop I went to geared toward self-empowerment or healing, every spiritual group I attended around men's work, meditation, developing consciousness or awareness, I shared relevant pieces of my story, my growth, the lessons I learned, and my healing. Every time, I had individuals approach me after the event or during breaks to thank me, hug me, and tell me what I shared had a deep impact on them.

In *Power vs. Force,* David Hawkins writes that when we heal ourselves we are also healing the collective, and we are healing others around us. We begin vibrating on a higher level as we move out of the energy of resentment, limitation, or unworthiness and we step into the energy of forgiveness, compassion, empowerment, and purposefulness. Those around us and those we maintain relationships with can feel this shift, and it has a tangible effect on them. As we change and grow, we demonstrate to others through our example of how to change and grow. In classes, I have listened as others shared that when we heal the wounds from those dynamics in ourselves, we are healing those same wounds in our parents, our grandparents, and others who have come before us and experienced the same. We also are healing this in the generations that will follow, putting an end to the toxic dynamics. Engaging in this healing work is a form of conscious service because countless others benefit from our work.

While we may not have a tangible awareness of it, this form of service creates a ripple effect that emanates from us. When we share our experiences with others and they thank us, we know there was some beneficial impact on them. They may have learned a lesson for themselves. They may have received some insight to facilitate their own healing, or they may have released some pain buried within them. They will move out into the world carrying the positive energy of the interaction with them, and it will be shared with others we do not even know.

This is oneness in action. Our energy, our intentions, and our healing experiences are carried forward, expressed in the world and in the experiences of countless individuals. We likely will never meet or encounter most of the people we have an impact on.

One of my father figures from our Men's Ministry shared a story with me of the indirect impact I had on someone else's life through my sharing. He is a psychiatrist who works with individuals who come into a homeless shelter. I had shared with our men's group the realizations I had around my own fears of loneliness and isolation and of how this operated behind my compulsions to get involved in romantic relationships with women. I shared how this fear resulted in a high risk for attracting unhealthy partners and how I often remained in relationships in which abuse and neglect were prominent or where my needs or preferences were not being met.

Several months later, this psychiatrist and I were having dinner with one another. He shared with me that he had a female patient repeatedly communicating serious issues she was having in a romantic relationship with a partner who was an alcoholic and physically abusive. She seemed unable or unwilling to set healthy boundaries for herself or to leave the relationship. He told me that he shared with her my story of feeling stuck in my second marriage, even though Anna was emotionally abusive and even violent toward me. He also told her of the realizations I had about why I did not feel I could maintain my own boundaries or leave my relationships. He shared with her how it felt more comfortable for me to remain in an unhealthy relationship than to be alone. He proceeded to tell me that several weeks later, this patient returned to him. She thanked him for shining a light on this same characteristic within her, and through her realization, she was able to heal enough to walk away from her abusive partner.

This is the ripple effect, and these are the types of possibilities that exist through our authentic sharing with others. It is a demonstration that as we heal ourselves, we also heal those around us.

My Discovery and Use of Writing as a Gift

Another significant gift revealed to me, one that caught me by surprise, is my ability to express myself in writing. I did not know I was a writer, and I did not know I enjoyed writing. I just started doing it to help me process my healing work. Most of the realizations I had that were necessary for my own healing came to me through writing. I did much of my emotional processing and released a lot of repressed pain through writing. I started sharing my writing with others as a means to be open and authentic, and, to my surprise, many of the people I shared with gave me the same feedback: "You are a gifted writer."

Opening myself to this gift and allowing it to flow led me to the realization that I needed to write this book. In line with Tama Kieves' quote above, I believe I am called to share my story with as many individuals as I can who are receptive to hearing it. I believe I can help countless people recover from their own experiences of abuse, wherever the effects still linger in their life circumstances. This book is a product of my belief and of my intentions. The more I wrote, and the more I envisioned this process unfolding, the stronger the fire within me grew. As this process unfolded, I learned that the identification and embodiment of my purpose were born from the recognition of my own gifts and from setting a deliberate intention to use them to benefit others.

My writing also served another beneficial purpose in my experience related to my journey toward practitioner training. One of the primary commitments practitioners make is to offer prayer support to those who seek it. I am now licensed as a practitioner, and I have been offering prayer support to others from the moment I began witnessing the effects of prayer in my experiences. I already had a regular practice of writing my own spiritual mind treatments in my journals. Therefore, I began writing prayers for others who asked me for prayer support. I quickly learned I have a great passion for writing prayers for others, and it is another avenue to express my love of writing.

I have found new ways to do this as a practitioner. I have provided dozens of people with written prayers, and I maintain this practice with several dedicated prayer partners—individuals with whom I maintain relationships for the purpose of providing one another regular prayer support. I have been so blessed to learn from some of these people that my prayers had such an impact on them that they printed them out, taped them to their refrigerators, or placed them on their altars to reread as they navigated a particular challenge. I find it deeply fulfilling to know I have used my gifts in a way to help and benefit those I care about.

We all have innate unique gifts and abilities. Some of them are hidden or buried beneath repressed pain. What I know now from my own experience is if we set a conscious intention and we believe those gifts and abilities are revealed to us, and if we believe opportunities come into our experience to use them to benefit others, then results appear. The realizations occur, the opportunities come into our lives, and then we get the chance to make a difference and to contribute.

It is easy to look out into the world and see countless problems. It is easy to feel overwhelmed and latch onto a belief that an individual can't possibly make a difference. There are wars, hunger, homelessness, abuse, violence, greed, pollution, mental illness, natural disasters, environmental catastrophes, and so much more happening. However, there also are countless good people, awake people, conscious people out in the world doing good work and showing up as beneficial presences constantly. We have a song we sing at our church that speaks to this: "I cannot do all the good that the world needs, but the world needs all the good that I can do."

You are not responsible for fixing and resolving every single problem in the world. Identify your gifts, find ways you enjoy using them to benefit others, and begin engaging in activities that allow you to improve and contribute. This is enough, and every contribution helps the collective.

Know that sharing your healing journey is one of the most impactful ways you can contribute. Also, know there are countless others who are awake, who have the perfect gifts within them, and who are working with deliberate intention right now to resolve issues that are not yours to address.

Do your healing work, and then begin showing up as a beneficial presence in the world through conscious service. Your service heals others, heals the world, and continues to heal you. This has been the most rewarding piece of my own healing journey, and I wish for each of you to experience the same blessings in your lives as I have by choosing to use my gifts for good.

AFTERWORD

Closure: Our Next Generation

 Abuse can be generational. Every individual I have spoken with who was abused as a child has reported that their parents also experienced abuse or trauma as children. The same is true for my parents. Essentially, the limiting beliefs, the habitual emotional reactions, and the behavioral patterns get projected onto the next generation, being passed down from the previous generation to the next. Abuse of others becomes a coping mechanism to deal with limiting beliefs and the repressed emotions, and it is a learned behavior, carried forward. My mother always said to me, "You do what you know until you know better." However, eventually, one of us must wake up and stop the cycle.

 The children of this next generation are highly gifted, highly aware, and exhibit amazing intuition and emotional maturity. I am shocked at the behaviors I observe in my own children and at the level of awareness and emotional maturity they possess. My older son, Dillon, is a highly gifted intuitive empath. There have been five times in my life now when I have been heavily thinking about some major decision, then he has blurted out some statement at a random time completely relevant to my thoughts. This has occurred too many times now to be coincidence. I have observed him reading or discerning the emotional state of others around him, even adults. He picks up emotions from other children close to him like a sponge.

There was a time when I overreacted toward him because he was lying to me about an incident. I observed him over several weeks taking toys away from his younger brother, and then not even playing with them. He was just hiding them from his brother, and, naturally, his brother was upset. I tried repeatedly to reprimand him, put him in timeouts, take toys away from him in my efforts to stop this behavior. Nothing seemed to be working, and I did not understand the behavior, especially when he started lying about it. I tried to understand his behavior from Thomas Hora's model of anger, in which he states, "All anger is wanting or not wanting." But I could not figure out what he wanted. One of my prayer partners explained to me that she and her younger sister had a similar age gap between them as my children do. She explained her parents had to devote more time and attention toward the younger sister, so the older sister became jealous because of perceived neglect or lack of attention. She started lashing out at her younger sister—bullying her, taking toys away, etc. What she wanted was more attention from the parents.

I went home and shared this story with Dillon—not the conclusion, just the story. I asked him what he thought of it. He immediately said, "Yes, Dad, that's it. This is why I have been taking toys away from my younger brother. You have to spend a lot of time with him, and I get upset and do not feel like I get enough time with you."

During this time, I was potty training my younger son, Michael, and I still had to bathe him, prepare all of his meals, and fulfill all the other responsibilities that came with parenting a toddler. There was a vast difference in the time and attention I could give to my two boys. I was amazed Dillon arrived at this conclusion all on his own, being eight years old at the time. I then owned my part for overreacting to him when he lied to me about hiding his brother's toys. I shared with him that I had been lied to quite a bit in my life, and I had an individual tell lies about me in an attempt to get me into trouble because this person was carrying so much resentment toward me. My son immediately stated, "OK, I understand. Someone else lied to you a lot and told lies about you. Then when someone new lies to you, the hurt just gets put onto the new person." Again, this coming from an eight-year-old child. He was absolutely correct.

Michael also has exhibited similar behaviors. I struggled with him in his earlier years related to healthy eating. (I am sure there are many parents who can relate.) There was a variety of healthy foods he would eat without resistance when he was two. Then suddenly, he began boycotting them all and became quite demanding about what he wanted to eat—items which were not healthy choices. I would present him with options, and he would throw raucous temper tantrums because he could not eat peanut butter for dinner. It got to the point where I was not allowing him to eat anything until he chose to have some healthy option he ate in the past. It turned into a standoff one weekend. He cried, screamed, and threw tantrums, and this went on for more than five hours. I did not give in. However, the self-doubt rose to a high level within me. I began questioning myself, whether I was being too hard on him, whether my tough stance was warranted. Eventually, he ate something healthy and then got to enjoy other favorite foods.

What amazed me from this incident was that shortly after this five-hour standoff—when he was crying, screaming, and shouting—he thanked me. We were driving to run some errands afterward, and again I was mulling over the self-doubt and wondering if I had been too hard on him. Then he just blurted out from the back seat in the middle of our drive. "Thank you, Daddy." I was in such shock, I simply said, "What?" He repeated, "Thank you, Daddy." I have never had any comparable standoffs with him around any circumstances since.

I have heard similar stories from other parents with children around the same age as mine. Their intuition, discernment, and awareness of what is going on around them and in the world is shocking at times. These kids coming up in this generation are highly gifted and well connected. The abuse I experienced was primarily aimed at squashing and repressing my emotions, and it is crucial we not carry this forward or the gifts these kids demonstrate will become repressed—the same as mine were.

We have to allow them and encourage them to share their thoughts and feelings. We have to listen to them. The philosophy I grew up with, "Children are seen but not heard," needs to be discarded and never looked at again. We must allow our children to openly express what they are thinking, and we must teach them how to allow emotions to pass through them in healthy ways. If we allow our children to feel their emotions and be comfortable expressing them, they will never learn the detrimental habit of repression. They will never learn the unhealthy dynamic of invalidating someone else's feelings.

Most importantly, they will be able to feel and recognize Spirit communicating to them through their own feelings. They will learn compassion. They will learn to trust their intuition. They will learn to listen to their hearts. They will be far more tuned into their inner compass than many of us were, given our circumstances growing up. They will make a great difference in this world.

I personally cannot wait to see how my sons develop their gifts that I have recognized in them at such young ages. I encourage my children to talk about and share the experiences they have when their gifts show up. I want them to be aware of their own gifts, and I want them to understand them. I want them to feel these gifts and recognize them operating in their lives. Mostly, I want to see the great potential that can come when their gifts are encouraged rather than repressed. I want to see what can bloom from their gifts once the kids grow up and begin expressing themselves.

We have miracles to witness through these kids of ours, and we have to do our part to keep the gifts flowing and developing so they can be shared with the world at their greatest potential.

BIBLIOGRAPHY

Ashley-Farrand, Thomas, *Healing Mantras: Using Sound Affirmations for Personal Power, Creativity, and Healing.* New York: Ballantine Wellspring, the Random House Publishing Group, 2008.

[Buddha], *The Dhammapada*: translated with an introduction and notes by John Ross Carter and Mahinda Palihawadana. New York: Oxford University Press, 1998.

Chopra, Deepak M.D., *Creating Health: How to Wake Up the Body's Intelligence.* New York: Houghton Mifflin Company, 1987.

———. *The Spontaneous Fulfillment of Desire: Harnessing the Infinite Power of Coincidence.* New York: Harmony Books, Member of the Crown Publishing Group, a Division of Random House, 2003.

Dispenza, Dr. Joe, *Breaking the Habit of Being Yourself: How to Lose Your Mind and Create a New One.* Carlsbad, California, Hay House, 2012.

Grenny, Joseph, *Crucial Skills Newsletter.* VitalSmarts, May 1, 2018.

Gottman, John M., M.D., and Joan DeClaire, *The Relationship Cure: A 5-Step Guide to Strengthening Your Marriage, Family, and Friendships.* New York: Three Rivers Press, 2001.

Hawkins, David R., M.D., Ph.D., *Power vs. Force: The Hidden Determinants of Human Behavior.* Carlsbad, California: Hay House, 2002.

Hemmingway, Ernest, *A Farewell to Arms.* New York: Charles Scribner's Sons, 1929.

Holmes, Ernest, *How to Use the Science of Mind Principles in Practice.* Golden, Colorado: Science of Mind Publishing, 1950.

———, *The Science of Mind.* New York: Penguin Group, 1938.

Hora, Thomas, M.D., *One Mind.* Old Lyme, Connecticut: The PAGL Foundation, 2001.

Jennings, Rev. Jesse, *The Essential Ernest Holmes: Collected Writings by the Author of The Science of Mind.* New York: Jeremy P. Tarcher/Putman, a member of Penguin Putnam, Inc., and The United Church of Religious Science, 2002.

Kieves, Tama, *Inspired and Unstoppable: Wildly Succeeding in Your Life's Work.* New York: Jeremy P. Tarcher/Penguin, a Member of Penguin Group, 2012.

McTaggart, Lynne, *The Intention Experiment: Using Your Thoughts to Change Your Life and the World.* New York: Atria Paperback, a Division of Simon & Schuster, 2013.

Myss, Caroline, *Entering the Castle: Finding the Inner Path to God and Your Soul's Purpose.* New York: Free Press, a Division of Simon & Schuster, 2007.

Rankin, Lissa, M.D., *Mind Over Medicine: Scientific Proof that You Can Heal Yourself.* Carlsbad, California: Hay House, 2013.

Ruiz, Don Miguel, *The Four Agreements: A Practical Guide to Personal Freedom.* San Rafael, California: Amber Allen Publishing, 1997.

Stanfield, Jana, *All the Good: Let the Change Begin.* Relatively Famous Records, 2003.

Teel, Rev. Roger, D.D., *This Life Is Joy: Discovering the Spiritual Laws to Live More Powerfully, Lovingly, and Happily.* New York: Tarcher Perigee, an Imprint of Penguin Random House, 2014.

Tolle, Eckhart, *The Power of Now: A Guide to Spiritual Enlightenment.* Vancouver, British Columbia, and Novato, California: Namaste Publishing and New World Library, 1999.

Vyasa, *The Bhagavad-Gita.* Chicago, Illinois: The University of Chicago Press, 1929.

ABOUT THE AUTHOR

Christopher Paul Russell is a licensed practitioner of Religious Science (RScP) in his home spiritual community at Mile Hi Church in Lakewood, Colorado. He completed his practitioner training and licensure in June of 2021.

He has dedicated his entire spiritual journey and healing path to transcending the effects of his own history of child abuse and neglect for a larger purpose of helping others along their healing journeys, especially those who have been through similar experiences. He passionately maintains a belief and faith that if all of humanity recognizes and embodies the inherent truth of who and what we truly are—spiritual beings with all the attributes of the Divine at our core—then all forms of household abuse, trauma, neglect, and domestic violence would come to an end. He also believes this process is unfolding all around us here and now, and he has chosen to use his newly discovered gift of writing to do his part to bring this about.

Russell is a single father to two boys and enjoys sharing a variety of outdoor recreational activities that Colorado and the Rocky Mountains have to offer—cycling, skiing, hiking, camping, canoeing, fishing, and hunting. Professionally, he is a licensed professional engineer with the Colorado Department of Transportation, Soils & Geotechnical Program, with fifteen years of experience in the industry of geotechnical/geological engineering. In his mind and still in his heart, he is a soil and rock nerd who loves working in the combined field of geological science and transportation infrastructure.

He is excited to see what doors open and what opportunities flow in with his new endeavors of engaging in practitioner service and also as a newly published author. Visit http://christopherpaulrussell.com/ to learn more about him as he embarks on this new phase of his life.

www.ingramcontent.com/pod-product-compliance
Lightning Source LLC
Chambersburg PA
CBHW071655090426
42738CB00009B/1534